WORKBOOK

IN

AMERICAN HISTORY

Cover Photo: Paul Revere, silversmith and craftsman
Painting by John Singleton Copley. *(Courtesy of Museum of Fine Arts, Boston, Massachusetts)*

ISBN 1-881-089-339 (Volume I)

Telephone Orders: 1-800-345-1776

PRINTED IN THE UNITED STATES OF AMERICA

Fifth Printing 2004

Contents

Succeeding in History Courses

by John McClymer

STUDYING HISTORY AND STUDYING FOR EXAMS

The instructor who designed this course hopes you will take advantage of the opportunity to learn about the American past. Your own objectives in taking the course may be somewhat different. You may be taking it because it fulfills some requirement for graduation or because it fits into your schedule or, perish the thought, because it seems less objectionable than the alternative you could be taking.

In a better world, these differences between your objectives and those of the course would not matter. The studying you do to perform well on exams and papers would involve your learning a fair amount of history. And so your grade would certify that you had indeed left the course with a more informed and thoughtful understanding of the American past than you had when you entered it. Unhappily, in the world we must actually live in, the connection between studying history and studying for exams in history is not necessarily so clear or straightforward.

The hard fact is that many students manage to prepare themselves for mid-terms and finals without permanently adding to their understanding. There they sit, yellow hi-liting pens in hand, plodding through the assigned chapters. Grim-faced, they underline every declarative sentence in sight. Then they trace and retrace their tracks trying to commit every yellowed fact to memory. As the time of the test draws near, they choke back that first faint feeling of panic by trying to guess the likeliest question. The instructor is never, they say to themselves, going to ask us to identify George Washington. But what about Silas Deane? And Pinckney? No, wait. There were TWO Pinckneys! That means there is almost certainly going to be a question about ONE of them. So it is that some students devote more energy to Thomas and Charles Cotesworth Pinckney than they do to George Washington. By such tactics they may get ready for the exam, but sabotage their chance of gaining any insight into American history.

Life does afford worse tragedies. This one, however, is remediable. And this appendix can help. It is designed to help you do well in the course, and to help you learn some history. It is, in fact, dedicated to the proposition that the easiest and most satisfying way to succeed in a history course is to learn some history. It makes very little sense, after all is said and done, to spend your time trying to keep the Pinckneys straight or running down a fact or two about Silas Deane. What will it profit you? You may pick up a few points on the short answer section of the exam, but those few points are a small reward for hours of studying. And, in the meantime, your essay on Washington as a political leader was distinctly mediocre. Clearly something is wrong.

That something is that studying for exams is a poor way of learning history. On the other hand, studying history is an excellent way of preparing for exams. If you had, for example, thought about American relations with France during John Adams' presidency, you would very probably remember who Charles C. Pinckney was. And you would scarcely have had to memorize anything.

The object of this essay is to persuade you to make some changes in the way you study. The first is to conserve your yellow pens. All that hi-liting simply lowers the resale value of the book. If you underline everything you read, you will wind up with a book of underlinings. There may be some psychological comfort in that. All of that yellow does provide visible evidence that you read the material. Unfortunately, it will not leave you with a useful guide to what to review. You have hi-lited too much.

A second drawback follows from the first. You have created a democracy of facts. All names, dates, and events are equally yellow. The Pinckneys and Silas Deane, in other words, have just become as noteworthy as George Washington or John Adams. You need, more than anything else, some way of determining what is important.

The next step may prove harder. You will have to give up trying to learn history by rote. A certain amount of memorizing may be unavoidable in a survey course, but ultimately it is the enemy of understanding. That is because many people use it as an alternative to thinking. Have you ever wished there were a better way? Well, there is. If you understand what Lincoln had hoped to accomplish with the Emancipation Proclamation, for example, you will not need to memorize its provisions. You will know why it did not promise freedom to any of the slaves in states (like Maryland or Missouri) which remained loyal to the Union. You will know why the Proclamation did not go into effect until one hundred days after it was issued. You will not, in short, stumble over a question like: "Whom did the Emancipation Proclamation emancipate?"

Facts are by no means unimportant. It is essential to have something to think about. But it is generally more fun to pay attention to ideas. Lincoln, to pursue this example, was interested above all else in restoring the Union. He was perfectly willing, he said, to keep slavery if that would accomplish his purpose; he was equally willing to abolish slavery if that would do the trick. So there is no mystery that in the Emancipation Proclamation he gave the states of the Confederacy one hundred days to return to the Union on pain of losing their slaves if they did not. The same reason explains why the Proclamation did not apply to slave states still in the Union.

If you take care of the ideas, the facts will assemble themselves. There are two reasons for this happy state of affairs. One has to do with the way in which textbooks are written and courses taught. The other has to do with the way people learn.

No historian, including the authors of the text and your instructor, pretends that history is the story of everything that ever happened. Obviously, many things happened for which there are no surviving records. More importantly, scholars use the records that have survived in a highly selective way. Even though they are always interested in finding new information, and in finding new ways of using information already known, each individual work of history—be it an article, a doctoral dissertation, a monograph, a textbook, a course of lectures—represents hundreds and thousands of choices about what to include and what to omit. Much more is known, for example, about the signers of the Declaration of Independence than you will read in any textbook. What you actually encounter in this course, as a result, is here because the text authors or your teacher decided for some reason to include it. Usually the reason is that this particular bit of information helps explain or illustrate some pattern of behavior or thought. The moral for you should be clear. Focus on these patterns. They are what you should be thinking about.

If you do, learning theorists have some good news for you. They have found that while it is difficult for the average person to recall disconnected bits of data (for example, which Pinckney was an emissary to France during the XYZ affair), it is comparatively easy to remember details of coherent stories. This is not a very startling finding. Details make sense once you see how they fit together. Let us return to the example of the Emancipation Proclamation. Lincoln's actions followed from: 1) his political priorities in which the integrity of the Union outranked achieving peace or ending slavery, 2) his analysis of the course of the war, and, 3) his perception of the choices open to him. Had Lincoln valued peace or ending slavery more highly than the Union, had easy victory or actual defeat seemed near at hand, had other inducements to the states of Confederacy to return to the Union seemed more promising, he would have acted differently. Once Lincoln's perception of the situation becomes clear to you, you will have little, if any, difficulty remembering what he did.

Neither compulsive underlining nor prodigious memorization will help you to understand these patterns. What will? We can rephrase the question: What does it mean to read and listen intelligently? For most of us, reading and listening are passive forms of behavior. We sit and wait to be told. Someone else, we expect, will provide the answers. Worse, we expect someone else will provide the questions. And, of course, they do. For our part, we limit ourselves to hi-liting and jotting notes. At best, this situation leaves us with a more or less adequate record of what someone else thinks we should know.

Most of what passes for studying involves not a conscientious effort to wrestle with the subject, but a determined effort to be prepared to answer likely questions. That is why we pay more heed to Silas Deane than to George Washington. It is why studying for exams is such a poor way to learn history. And, its chief drawback perhaps from your point of view, it is usually a recipe for earning a mediocre grade.

Letting your teacher or the authors of the text do your thinking for you also leads to tedium. The simple truth is that passivity is boring. Yet we rarely blame ourselves for being bored. It can not be our own fault. We are only "taking" the course. Someone else is "giving" it, and so we look to the instructor to liven things up a bit. Maybe some audio-visuals or a bit of humor, we think, would make the course less dreary. These hopes are misplaced for, while humor is a blessed thing and audio-visuals have their place, it is the nitty-gritty of the course that should interest us.

Boredom is almost always a self-inflicted wound. Students are bored because they expect the instructor to be interesting when it is they who must themselves take an interest. Teacher and students are equally responsible for the success of a course. Most of the students in American history courses will live out the rest of their lives in the United States. Their lives will be affected for both good and ill by what has happened in the American past. It follows that the simple desire to make sense of their own lives should lead them to take an interest in this course.

Taking an interest involves learning to read and listen actively. Intellectual activity begins with questions—Your own questions directed, in the first instance, to yourself and then to your teacher. Why is it, you might wonder, that the United States is the only industrialized country without a comprehensive national system of health care? Why did slavery last so long in the American South? Why did the Founding Fathers establish a republic? And why did a party system develop even though the founders were bitterly opposed to political parties? Why, for that matter, were they so set against parties in the first place?

You will not always find satisfactory answers. But you will have started to think about the meaning of the American past. And when you do, something quite desirable happens to all of those facts. They will take on life and become evidence, clues to the answers you are seeking. The questions, that is, will give you a rational basis for deciding which facts are important. And George Washington will finally receive his well-deserved priority over the Pinckneys.

All of this leads directly to the question of how you should study for this course. It is a truism that students do poorly when they are ill-prepared. But we too easily assume that the sole reason why we are sometimes ill-prepared is because we did not spend enough time getting ready. This is a half-truth, and a dangerous one. It ignores the critical fact that we often use the time we spend reviewing very inefficiently. And, since there is often no practical way of increasing the time we have to review (there being, after all, only so many working hours in the day), it makes far more sense to use the time we do have effectively instead of moaning about how we should have studied more.

How do you get ready for an exam? Do you get out your textbook and notes and pour over them again and again until the time runs out or the sheer boredom of it all crushes your good intentions? If so, then you have lots of company—a consolation of sorts. There is, on the other hand, a better way.

Find a quiet and comfortable spot (something not always easy to do in a dormitory). Bring along a blank pad and something to write with. Then jot down, just as they occur to you, whatever items you can remember about the course. Do not rush yourself. And do not try, at this stage, to put things in order. Just sit there and scribble down whatever pops into your mind. After a while you will have quite a large and varied mix of names, ideas, dates and events. Then see how much of this you can put together. There is no need to write out whole sentences or paragraphs. An arrow or a word or two will frequently be enough. You are not, after all, going to hand these scribbles in. You are just collecting your thoughts. Do not be concerned if this process seems to be taking up some of the limited time you have to study. It will prove to be time well spent.

Now look over what you have written. Where are the gaps? You will find that you know a fair bit about the material just from your previous reading of the text and from listening in class. But some topics will still be obscure. You may, for example, pretty well understand why Polk declared war on Mexico, but you may feel less sure about his negotiations with Great Britain over Oregon. All right. Now you know what you should be studying. There is no reason for you to go over the war with Mexico. Why study what you already know. And here is the nub of the matter, for an intelligent review is one that focuses on what you need to refresh your mind about.

You will doubtless have noticed that this strategy presupposes that you have read the textbook and taken good notes in class. Just what, you might wonder, are good notes? Many students think that the closer they come to transcribing the instructor's every word the better their notes are. They are mistaken. There are several reasons why. Unless your shorthand is topnotch, you will not succeed. Instead you will be frantically scrambling to catch up. In the process you will not only miss some of what is said, but you will pay attention to scarcely any of the lecture. At the end of class you will have: 1) a sore hand; 2) a great deal of barely legible notes; and 3) little if any idea of what the class was about.

Another reason not to attempt to transcribe lectures (taping them, by the way, is usually a poor idea) is that you will spend much of your time taking down information you either already know or can easily find in the textbook. How often do you need to see the fact that Jefferson Davis was the president of the Confederacy? A sensible person will decide once is enough.

The most important reason not to take down everything is that it prevents you from doing what you ought to be doing during class, listening intelligently. Your instructor is not simply transmitting information during a lecture but is also seeking to explain the hows and whys of the American past. It is these explanations you should be listening for, and your notes should focus on them. It is much easier to do this if you have read the relevant textbook chapters first. That way you will already know much of the factual information. And you will have, one hopes, some questions already in your mind. You will have, that is, something to listen for. And you can take notes sensibly. You can fill in explanations of points that had puzzled you, jot down unfamiliar facts, and devote most of your time to listening instead of writing. Your hand will not be sore; you will know what the class was about; and your notes will complement rather than duplicate what you already knew.

So far we have dealt mainly with the mechanics of studying—taking notes, reviewing for exams, and the like. Valuable as knowing the mechanics can be, and in terms of your grade they can be very valuable indeed, the real secret to studying history is learning how to think historically. History is both a body of knowledge about the past and a way of thinking about the human condition. You are probably familiar with the first of these two aspects of the subject. History is knowing about the Revolution, the Civil War, and so on. It is knowing, that is, that they happened, when they happened, and how they happened. It is also having some explanation of why they happened as they did, and of the differences their happening made. All of that is undoubtedly perfectly obvious to you. It may, in fact, seem to include the sum and substance of history. It does not.

History is also a way of thinking. It rests on the assumption that you understand what something is by finding out how it came to be that way. This is an assumption which, consciously or not, you share. When you ask friends how they are doing, for example, you are really asking what has happened to them since you last met. You are asking about the past—the recent past to be sure—but the past nonetheless. You accept, that is, the axiom that the past has consequences for the present and the future. If your roommate has just failed an organic chemistry final, to use a sad but not uncommon occurrence, you both know what that will mean for her chances of getting into medical school.

You also know, if you think about it for a minute, that the political beliefs of the Founding Fathers still matter. They matter not only because their beliefs continue to influence our own but also because we continue to use them as the standard against which we measure present-day political figures. You can even appreciate that the child-rearing practices of the Puritans are worth knowing about—not of course because they have been passed down unchanged from the seventeenth century nor because they provide a model for you in raising your own family, but because we can not understand changing cultural realities or social practices unless we first have a clear idea of what they were once like. Change, in short, is incomprehensible if we do not have a point of reference from which to measure it. And history alone can provide us with such a fixed point.

Learning to think historically is a simple necessity if we hope to make sense of the world around us. Fortunately, it involves nothing more than learning to employ in a disciplined way the same patterns of thought we already use on a daily basis. That your roommate failed organic chemistry is a historical fact just as Lincoln's victory in the presidential election of 1860 is. How your roommate failed, and how Lincoln won, can also be determined factually, to some degree. You can, that is, discover which questions your roommate got wrong, just as you can find out which states Lincoln carried. You can even begin to assemble facts which will help explain why your roommate missed those particular questions and why Lincoln won those particular states. With regard to your roommate, you might recall that she cut a number of classes. You could hypothesize that some of the material covered in those classes was on the exam. You might recall that your roommate had a political science paper to finish the week before the exam. Perhaps that kept her from studying chemistry thoroughly.

Similarly you could determine with some accuracy which voting blocs went for Lincoln. You could then analyze the campaign issues and speculate about how those constituencies lined up on those issues. In both cases you would be trying to marshall the facts so that they would support some interpretation. Clearly, if you could know all of the facts, and if there were only one possible explanation for them, your interpretation would be true in the same way that the facts themselves are true. You could say: it happened this way and no other.

Unfortunately, life is not so amenable to explanation. You will never have all the facts, and no explanation will ever be the only one possible. Consider your roommate's "F" in organic. You know which questions were missed. But the questions on the exam could have been different. Then your roommate's grade would, possibly, have also been different. So knowing which questions your roommate lost points on is not enough. You would also have to know why these particular questions, and not others, were on the test in the first place. Consider too that the test scores were probably "curved." A more forgiving curve might have allowed your roommate to pass. But to know why the curve was the way it was you would have to know why the other raw scores were the way they were. Your roommate's raw score, the actual points lost on particular questions, in other words, is only half the story. That score could, presumably, have become an "A" if other students in the course had done even worse than your roommate. There is no need to pursue the point any farther. It is clear that you could never be sure you knew all of the relevant facts. And if this be true for your roommate's "F", how much more obviously true it must be for Lincoln's election. There were millions of voters. Who could know why they all voted as they did?

Despite all of this you may feel—and quite sensibly—that your roommate's "F" is hardly an impenetrable enigma. You may not know everything about it, but you know enough. You can offer an explanation that fits the facts you do know and is congruent with what you know of your roommate's study habits, general intelligence, and so forth. What you have is an interpretation. So too with Lincoln's election. People may have had reasons for voting as they did that you will never know, but you can supply enough reasons to explain why he won. You can explain, that is, what is known, and your view is compatible with what is known about American elections during that period.

You can perhaps already see how to define a convincing interpretation. It is one that provides that simplest sensible account of why something happened. The goal of historical inquiry is interpretation. And while, as we have seen, interpretation is not synonymous with truth, it is something more than mere opinion.

Anyone can have an opinion. People claim that have a right to have opinions about anything and everything (some even seem to feel it is their duty to have an opinion about everything). But you have to earn the right to offer an interpretation because an interpretation is a thoughtful explanation based on a careful assessment of evidence. It follows that when you find scholars disagreeing over how to interpret the American Revolution, say, as Professors McDonald and Genovese do in one of their debates, you ought not to conclude that their dispute is "just a matter of opinion" or that the truth probably lies somewhere in the middle (an old saw that should be

permanently retired) or that one opinion (yours included) is just as good as another. Rather you need to ask: how well do these interpretations accord with what I know about the Revolution? How much sense can I make of what happened before and after it by using one or another of these explanations? The debates, in short, are an invitation to you to think about the meaning of American history. They should prompt you to struggle with the issues in your own mind and to come up with your own interpretation.

You may feel somewhat hesitant about putting your own interpretation forward, particularly if it differs markedly from those offered by your instructor or the authors of the text. And, within limits, you should be hesitant. A certain intellectual modesty is becoming in a beginning student. But you have read the material; you have listened intelligently in class; and you have thought about the issues. So you have the right to a view of your own. Teaching is not indoctrination. The object of the course is not to tell you what to think. The goal is to help you learn to think for yourself. You are therefore entitled to disagree.

When presenting your own interpretation, whether or not it agrees with one you have already encountered, you should always explain clearly how you reached that particular conclusion. This means explaining what evidence you found most important; it means explaining why that evidence struck you as important; and it means explaining the logic of your position. If you can do these three things, then you need not fear presenting your own ideas.

This appendix has an additional feature designed to help you think about how historical interpretations are developed and tested. This is a section on how to read the McDonald-Genovese debates. You will quickly realize, as you read the debates, that McDonald and Genovese rarely disagree over the facts of American history. They disagree over which facts are important and over how they should be interpreted. This section contains suggested exercises you can do on your own, or which your instructor can assign, that will enable you to read the debates more critically.

It is now time to see how these general considerations about studying history apply to specific tasks you will have to undertake in this course. We will start with how to take midterm and final examinations.

HOW TO TAKE EXAMS

In the best of all possible worlds examinations would hold no terrors. You would be so well prepared that no question, no matter how tricky or obscure, could shake your serene confidence. Unfortunately, the real world normally finds the average student in a different situation. Somehow it seems one's preparation is always less than complete. And so one approaches exams with some anxiety. "Of course," one says to oneself, "I should have studied more. But I did not. Now what?" This section can not tell you how to get A's without studying, but it can suggest some practical steps which can help you earn the highest grade compatible with what you do know.

The first step is to look over the entire exam before you start answering any of it. It is impossible to budget your time sensibly until you know what the whole exam looks like. And if you fail to allow enough time for each question, two things— both bad—are likely to happen. The first is that you may have to leave some questions out, including perhaps some you might have answered very effectively. How often have you muttered: "I really knew that one!"? The other unhappy consequence is that you may have to rush through the last part of the exam. Again, there may be questions you could have answered very well if you had had more time.

How do you budget your time effectively? The idea, after all, is to make sure that you have enough time to answer fully all the questions you do know. So the best plan is also the simplest. Answer those questions first. It may feel a bit odd at first answering question #7 before #4, but you will soon enough get used to it. And you will find that, if you still run out of time, you at least have the satisfaction of knowing you are rushing through or leaving out questions you could not have answered very well anyway. You will, in other words, have guaranteed that you will receive the maximum credit for what you do know.

There is another advantage to answering questions in the order of your knowledge instead of in the order asked. Most students are at least a little tense before an exam. If you answer the first several questions well, that tension will likely go away. As you relax, you will find it easier to remember names, dates, and other bits of information. Contrariwise, if you get off to a shaky start, that simple case of pre-exam jitters can become full-scale panic. Should that happen, you may have trouble remembering your own phone number, and your chances of recalling those facts which are just on the tip of your tongue will shrink to the vanishing point. Obviously, it is very important to get off to a good start. So do not trust to luck. Do not just hope the first couple of questions are easy. You can make sure you get off on the right foot by answering first whatever questions you are sure of.

Let us suppose you have gotten through everything you think you know on the exam and you still have some time left. What should you do? You can now try to pick up a few extra points with some judicious guessing. There is not much point to trying to guess with essay questions. In all probability you will write something so vague that you will not get any credit for it anyway. Rather you should try to score on the short-answer section. Some types of questions were made for shrewd guesswork. Matching columns are ideal. A process of elimination will often tell you what the answer has to be. Multiple choice questions are almost as good. Here too you can eliminate some of the possibilities. Most teachers feel obligated to give you a choice of four or five possible answers, but find it hard to come up with more than three that are plausible. So you can normally count on being able to recognize the one or two that are just there as padding.

Once you have narrowed the choices down to two or three, you are ready to make your educated guess. There are three rules. 1) Always play your hunches, however vague. Your hunch is based on something you heard or read even if you can not remember what it is. So go with it. 2) Do not take your time. If you can not think of the answer, just pick one and have done with it. 3) Try to avoid changing answers. There are a number of studies showing that you are more likely to change a right answer than to correct a wrong one.

Identifications are the type of short-answer question most resistant to guesswork. Unless you have a fairly strong hunch about the answer, you should leave this sort of question blank. The reason is that while it is true that an incorrect answer will cost you no more points than leaving the question out altogether, it is also true that an incorrect answer says something about the depths of your ignorance which a blank space does not. You want the exam as a whole to convey what you do know. Supplying a mass of misinformation usually creates a presumption that you do not know what you are talking about even on those sections of the exam when you really do. So be careful about wild guesses. They are almost sure to do more harm than good.

These suggestions are not substitutes for studying. They may, however, help you get the most out of what you know. They may, that is, spell the difference between a mediocre grade and a good one.

HOW TO WRITE BOOK REVIEWS

One goal of book reviews is to set forth clearly and succinctly who (if anyone) would benefit from reading the work in question. It follows that a good review indicates the scope of the book, identifies its point of view, summarizes its main conclusions, evaluates its use of evidence, and—where possible—compares the book with others on the subject.

It is highly likely that you have written book reviews in high school or in other college courses so it is important that you do not approach this kind of assignment with a false sense of security. It sounds easy, after all, to write a five-hundred-or-so word essay. And you have written lots of other reviews. But did those other reviews focus clearly on the questions a good review must address? If they did not, your previous experience is not going to prove especially helpful. It may even prove something of a handicap. You may have developed some bad habits.

Easily the worst habit is that of summarizing not the book's argument but its contents. Let us suppose you are reviewing a biography of George Washington. The temptation is to write about Washington rather than about the book. This is a sure path to disaster. Washington had, to put it mildly, an eventful career. You are certainly not going to do it justice in a few paragraphs. And you are not, in all probability, going to find that much that is fresh or interesting to say about him. Meanwhile you have ignored your primary responsibility which is to tell the reader whether this biography has anything fresh or interesting to say.

So you need to remind yourself as forcefully as possible that your job is to review the book and not the subject of the book. Does the book focus narrowly on Washington or does it also go into the general history of America during those years? Is the author sympathetic to Washington, tending to see things Washington's way? Does the writer attempt to psychoanalyze Washington or stick to political and military questions? Is there a firm command of the available evidence (this requires you, alas, to read the footnotes)? And, last but not least, does the author have something new to say about Washington and his times? If so, how well documented is this new interpretation?

It is less important to evaluate how well the author writes. While it is hard to imagine a poorly written novel that is still worth reading, it is common enough (unhappily) for important historical works to be written in a plodding fashion. So you should comment on the quality of the author's prose, but you should generally not make that an important part of your overall evaluation unless it is so good or so awful that it makes reading the work sheer bliss or unrelieved torture.

You should generally not comment on whether or not you enjoyed the book. That is undoubtedly an important consideration for you, but it is of little interest to anyone else. There are some occasions when you need to suffer in silence. This is one of them.

HOW TO SELECT A TERM PAPER TOPIC

Doing research, as you may already have had occasion to learn, is hard work. Worse yet, it is often boring. Typically it involves long periods of going through material that is not what you were looking for and is not particularly interesting. It also involves taking detailed and careful notes, many of which you will never use. These are the dues you must pay if you are ever to earn the excitement which comes when you finally find that missing piece of evidence and make sense of things.

Not everything about doing research is boring. Aside from the indescribable sensation of actually finding out what you wanted to know, there are also occasional happy accidents where you stumble across something which, while not relevant to your research, nonetheless pricks your imagination. Many a historian studying an old political campaign has read up on the pennant races or fashions or radio listings for that year. These are, as one scholar put it, oases in the desert of historical evidence. But, as he quickly added, no one crosses the desert just to get to the oasis. The truth of the matter is that you have to have a good reason for getting to the other side. This means a topic you are genuinely interested in.

The point cannot be overemphasized. If you have a question you really want to answer, you will find it much easier to endure the tedium of turning all those pages. You will have a motive for taking good notes and for keeping your facts straight. If you are not truly interested in your topic, on the other hand, you may be in trouble. You are going to be constantly tempted to take short-cuts. And even if you resist temptation, you are going to find it hard to think seriously about what you do find.

So the topic has to interest you. That, you may be thinking, is easy to say. But what if your interest in American history is less than compelling? What if, perish the thought, you do not give two figs about the whole American past? Are you then going to be stuck with some topic you could care little about? The answer is "No". "No," that is, unless it turns out that you have no curiosity about anything at all; and, if that is the case, you are probably dead already or nearly so. Anything that can be examined chronologically is fair game for the historian. There are histories of sports and of sciences, of sexual practices and jokes about them, of work and of recreation. It is odd, to say the least, that students so often choose to write of war, politics, and diplomacy even when their real interests lie elsewhere. If you use your imagination, you should be able to find a topic which you are genuinely interested in and which your teacher agrees merits serious study. This being true, you have no one to blame but yourself if you wind up writing on some question you are not passionately concerned with answering.

Once you have such a topic you need to find ways of defining it so that you can write an intelligent essay. "The Automobile in American Life" could well serve as the subject for a very long book. It is not going to work as a subject for a term paper, and for two compelling reasons. First, you could not possibly research so vast a topic in the time you have to work with. Second, your paper, however long, is not going to be of book length—in fact it is not likely to exceed 5,000 words. So you would be stuck with trying to compress an immense amount of information into a brief essay. The final product will be a disaster.

You need to focus on some aspect of the general topic which can be intelligently treated in the space and time you have to work with. Students usually look at this problem backwards. They complain about how long their papers have to be. They should complain about how short they have to be. Space is a luxury you normally can not afford. If you have done a fair amount of research on an interesting topic, your problem is going to be one of finding a way of getting all you have to say into your paper. Writing consists of choices about what you want to say. And if you have done your work properly, the hard choices involve deciding what to leave out.

"Fair enough," you may be thinking, "but I do not want to get stuck researching some minute bit of trivia, the 'gear shift level from 1940 to 1953,' for example. I want to study the automobile in American life." Here we come to the heart of the matter. Your topic must be narrowly defined so that you can do it justice, but it must also throw some light on the broad question that interested you in the first place. This is easier said than done, but it can be done. The trick is to decide just what it is about your topic—cars in this in-

stance—that really interests you. Cars are means of transportation, of course, but they are also examples of technology, status symbols, and much else besides. Because of the automobile, cities and suburbs are designed in ways very different from how they were when people traveled by trolley or train. Because of the automobile, even teenage dating patterns are what they are. Having a driver's license, and regular access to a car, has become a crucial part of growing up.

The point is that you have to think about your topic and then decide what aspect of it to examine. If you wind up doing a treatise on changing methods of changing tires, you have only yourself to blame. You could have been studying sex and sexism in automobile advertising.

HOW TO LOCATE MATERIAL

Once you have worked up an interesting and practical topic for your term paper, you are ready to begin your research. For many students this means ambling over to the library and poking around in the card catalog. This may not be the best way to begin because the librarians who catalog the library's holdings, while skilled professionals, cannot possibly anticipate the needs of every individual researcher. So they catalog books by their main subject headings and then include obvious cross-references. Much of what you need, on the other hand, may not be obvious. So, for example, if you are interested in the causes of the Civil War, you will have no trouble finding a title like Kenneth Stampp's *And The War Came* listed under "U.S. History, Civil War." But will you find Roy Nichol's *Disruption of the American Democracy*? You may not.

The point is that there may be a number of important works in your library you will not be able to find if you start by checking the card catalog. What should you do instead? The first thing is to locate the *Harvard Guide To American History*. This is an invaluable tool. It will tell you the best (in the editors' opinion) books and articles on your subject. For each title prepare a separate card listing full bibliographic specifics (i.e., the author's full name, the complete title including subtitle, the place of publication, the edition, and if a journal article the volume and issue numbers). You will need all of this information.

Now you have the beginnings of a decent bibliography. Your next step should be to introduce yourself to the research librarian. This person's specialty is helping people look for information. Yet many students never consult with a librarian. Do not pass up an opportunity to make your work easier! Ask your research librarian to help. Often he can point you to more specialized bibliograph- ical guides, can show you where to learn of the most recent books and articles, and can help you refine your topic by indicating what aspects are easiest to get information on.

You now have a reasonably extensive set of cards. And you can now safely consult the card catalog to see which of these titles your library has. Prepare yourself for some disappointments. Even good undergraduate libraries will not have everything you need. They will have some (un- less your library is very weak or your topic very esoteric). Virtually all college libraries participate in the inter-library loan system. This system, which the library staff will gladly explain to you, will permit you to get virtually any title you could wish for. The only catch is that you must give the library enough lead time. For books and articles which are not especially rare this normally means one to three weeks.

HOW TO TAKE NOTES

As you sift through the material you have found you will need to take careful notes. As you do, you should write down each piece of information which you believe might prove relevant on a notecard. You also will need to specify the full source for each piece of information.

If you follow these two bits of advice, you will save yourself much time and trouble. Finding in- formation the first time, in your sources, is trou- ble enough. You do not want to have to find it all over again when you sit down to write your pa- per. But this is often just what students have to do because they discover that they did not bother to write down some bit of data (which, perhaps, seemed only marginally important at the time) or because they took all of their notes on loose leaf paper and now must search through every page to find this one fact. It is far easier, over the long run, to have a separate card for each piece, or closely related pieces, of information. Tell your- self that you are the last of the big time spenders and can afford to use up index cards as though they were blank pieces of paper. After all, that is what they are.

The general rule is that you should take extra pains when compiling your research notes so that the actual writing will be as trouble-free as pos- sible. It follows from this that you should take lots of notes. Do not try to determine in advance whether or not you are going to use a particular bit of data. Always give yourself the benefit of the doubt. Similarly, do not try to decide in advance whether you will quote the source exactly or sim- ply paraphrase it. If you take down the exact words, you can always decide to make the idea your own by qualifying it in various ways and putting it in your own words. When taking notes, in brief, your motto should be: the more the merrier.

WRITING TERM PAPERS AND OTHER ESSAYS

You have no doubt already learned that next to mastery of the subject matter nothing is more im- portant for earning good grades than effective writing. You surely know people whose study habits are not all that they should be but whose grades are high. Nine times out of ten the secret of their success is their ability to write well. What they have to say may not always be all that im- pressive, but the way they say it is.

Students who are not among that relatively small group who write well sometimes think it unfair that writing skills should count so heavily. The course, some complain, is American History, not Creative Writing, and so their grade should not be influenced by their prose. Only what they know about history should count. But most teach- ers continue to believe that the ability to express what you know clearly and forcefully is an indis- pensable measure of how well you have learned the subject matter. So, like it or not, your writing is going to count. Writing well is an invaluable skill, and not only in college. Most good jobs (and most not-so-good ones) involve writing. There is correspondence, there are reports, there are memoranda. The writing will never stop.

No matter how poorly you write, you can learn to write effectively. This is not to say that anyone who desires it can become a brilliant prose styl- ist. Great talent is rare in every field. But anyone who can speak English effectively can learn to write it effectively. It is simply a matter of ex- pressing your ideas clearly. This you can learn to do. It does not require genius, merely patience and practice.

Charity, St. Paul said, was the chief of all the virtues. In expository prose, however, the chief virtue is clarity. And like charity, it covers a mul- titude of sins. Be they ever so humble, or homely, your sentences will receive a sympathetic read- ing if they are clear. Why? There are a number of reasons. The first is that your papers, reviews, and essays—while they may seem very long to you when writing them—are in reality quite brief. A twenty-page paper, for example, only contains 5,000 words. This means that you do not have very much space to get your ideas across. The less space you have, the more carefully you have to choose your words. If it takes you four or five pages to get to the point, you have wasted a substantial portion of your essay. (If, on the other hand, you were writing a 500 page book, those four or five pages would not matter so much.)

It has perhaps crossed your mind that there are occasions when you are not very eager to get to the point. Sometimes you may not be sure just what the point is. Sometimes you do know, but are not convinced that your point is a very good one. At such times, a little obfuscation may seem a better idea than clarity. It is not. I can assure you, based on my experience as a college teacher (which has involved reading thousands of student papers), there is nothing more troubling than reading a paper where the author tried to hedge bets or fudge ideas. The very worst thing you can do is leave it up to your reader (also known as your instructor) to decide what you are trying to say. Teachers, as a group, have not heeded St. Paul. They conspicuously lack charity when reading student papers. They will not give you the benefit of the doubt. They will, more often than not, decide that you did not get to the point because you do not know the material. We teachers can be a heartless breed. So, no matter how weak your ideas seem to you, set them forth clearly. Something is always better than nothing.

Clarity is a virtue in part because so many papers from other students will not exemplify it. As a result, your teacher will be inclined to read yours more sympathetically. What you said may not have been brilliant, but it did make sense. And, contrary to popular reports, most teachers really are interested in helping students. It is much easier to help you if your instructor can figure out what you were trying to say.

My mistakes will stand out, you are thinking. That sounds very dangerous. We have all been conditioned to avoid detection. The last thing we want is for the teacher to find out that we do not know something. But teachers delight in watching students improve. The reason is obvious: they see it as proof that they are doing a good job. They take special pleasure in the progress of students who start off poorly but steadily get better over the course of the semester. You can do a lot worse than be one of those students.

Let us assume that you are willing to give clarify a try. How do you go about writing clearly? The first rule of thumb is to avoid complexity. You should strive to write simply and directly. This does not mean that you are limited to a basic 1500-word vocabulary. There are hundreds of thousands of words in the language and you are entitled to use any of them, provided only that you use them correctly. You should not, on the other hand, go out of your way to find esoteric words or expressions. Use words that accurately express your meaning. Wherever possible use words that are part of your ordinary vocabulary. Above all, do not try to impress your instructor by using synonyms you located in a dictionary or, worse yet, a thesaurus. You run a high risk of using these words incorrectly because they may have connotations you are unaware of.

You should also avoid complicated grammatical structures. Do you know when to use the subjunctive mood? Do you know the rules about using semi-colons? Do you know which types of subordinate clauses require commas? If you have answered any or all of these questions negatively, then you should bone up on your grammar. And, in the meantime, you should avoid writing sentences where these kinds of questions arise. There is no reason to increase the probability of making an error. Grammatical errors can often be avoided simply by keeping your sentences fairly short. Qualifications of your main idea can go into separate sentences. You do not have to fit everything into a single sentence. Furthermore, your sentences will have more pace and rhythm if you keep them relatively short.

Grammatical difficulties—be they outright errors or merely negligent constructions—are a writer's nightmare. Each time you make an error or use an awkward phrase you distract the reader. He or she stops paying attention to what you are saying and instead focuses on how you are saying it. If you distract the reader often enough (four or five times a page will do it in most cases), you will have reduced your chances of getting your ideas across virtually to zero.

So it is vitally important to eliminate grammatical problems. This is, of course, easier said than done. But there are ways to do it. Many schools have writing centers where you can get help with your papers. If your school has such a center, use it. The improvement in both your prose and your G.P.A. can be dramatic. If your school lacks a writing workshop, ask your teacher to read over an early draft of your paper. This is the reader you have to please after all. So why not go straight to the source?

You may have observed that both of these suggestions presume that you will have completed an early draft. And so you should. But let us suppose that, like most college students, you write your papers by the dawn's early light just before they are due. You do not have an early draft. If you find yourself in this all-too-common situation, you may still be able to find someone who will, as a favor, read over your paper before you type the final version. There are college students who have a good working knowledge of grammar. You need to find one and get him or her to edit your work, that is, help you get rid of the most blatant errors. This person can also tell you if your paper is easy to follow. You should write so that someone unfamiliar with the subject but reasonably well informed in other respects can understand what you are saying. Such a person makes an excellent reader and can help you pinpoint the ideas you need to explain more fully.

Once you have worked out a scheme for eliminating grammatical shortcomings, you can turn to the equally crucial chore of articulating your ideas. This means deciding the most cogent sequence in which to present them, on the one hand, and explicating the connections between them on the other. The first order of business is making sure that your opening paragraphs clearly set out what your paper is about and how you are going to approach this topic. Your opening sentences should explain: what your topic involves; why it is worth investigating; and how you are going to look into it. If your topic were, for example, "Sex and Sexism in Automobile Advertising," you might write something like the following:

> The automobile is more than a means of transportation. It is also a powerful engine of change. Highways and suburbs have altered the human and physical geography of the nation. Shopping malls and drive-ins have transformed the retail economy. Social practices—from dating customs to recreational patterns—bear the imprint of the car. Cars have also come to symbolize status and prestige. Expensive models are perceived, and marketed, as visible signs of success. As a result, changing automotive advertising campaigns provide a wealth of data about how Americans have conceptualized the "good life" in this century.
>
> Success means different things to different people, but—if the car ads are to be believed—Americans tend to think of success in terms of power and sex.

You will note that this example sets the topic in a larger context, explains what the paper will examine (power and sex as components of the American idea of success), and how it will examine them (by analyzing changing patterns of automotive advertising). Further it explains why these ads are an important source of material for this topic.

"Well begun," the adage runs, "is half done." This is especially true in writing papers and essays. A good opening tells the reader what to expect. It piques curiosity and makes one eager to read on. A poor opening (one, that is, which leaves the reader still wondering what the paper is about or why a certain topic is important) does the opposite. So work on your openings! You may not have the time to write several drafts of your paper (although you should make the time), but you must take the time to rewrite your introduction as many times as necessary for it to sparkle.

You, as the author, have the responsibility of directing your reader's attention. You do this by explaining the logical connection(s) between the points you raise. You can not assume that your reader will figure out the logic of your paper. Your reader, you should recall, is a professional skeptic who starts from the assumption that you do not know what you are talking about. So it is the height of folly to assume that your instructor will supply logical connections for you. You have to supply them, and you do this—principally—by means of topic and transitional sentences.

Topic sentences introduce ideas. They belong at the beginning of paragraphs. All too often students bury their central ideas in the middle of paragraphs. Only the most attentive reader is likely to ferret them out. And while every teacher strives to be most attentive, the unvarnished truth of the matter is that there is usually a stack of papers to go through—a prospect that inspires a certain dread and tends to make one somewhat eager to get the whole business over with. So, despite our best intentions, we teachers are often less attentive than we should be. The lesson for you is clear. Do not risk having your best notions go unnoticed.

Transitional sentences explain connections. You can put them at the end of paragraphs if you wish. Wherever you put them, be sure you write them as carefully as you do your introduction and your topic sentences. A good topic sentence may also be a transitional device and improve the flow of your writing.

These few hints will not suffice to turn you into a good writer, but they can help you avoid fatal errors. If your writing is a problem, then you owe it to yourself to seek sustained professional help either in writing courses or at your school's writing center. Remember, a serviceable prose style will not only measurably improve your grade in this course (and many others), it will also improve your chances for success in whatever career you enter.

WHEN AND HOW TO USE FOOTNOTES

Many students apparently believe that the only thing worse than having to read footnotes is having to write them. It is easy to understand why they feel that way, but they are making much ado about very little. Footnotes are used to inform the reader (including your reader) where the information being used in the body of the paper can be found. That is the sum and substance of the matter.

So, when should you use a footnote? These are two occasions when you must. The first is when you are referring to someone's exact words whether by direct quotation or by paraphrase. The second is when you are referring to some bit of information that is not already well known or is someone's interpretation of the facts. How, you might wonder, can you tell whether or not something is already well-known? There is, fortunately, a simple rule. Any thing you can find in a standard textbook (like *Firsthand America*) does not need to be footnoted. Hence, for example, you do not need to footnote that George Washington was the first president of the United States. You do need to footnote an exact quotation from his "Farewell Address." You do not need to footnote that Henry Ford introduced the assembly line to the manufacture of automobiles. You do need to footnote your source for his political opinions.

As you can see from these examples, there is no mystery about using footnotes. If you are in doubt about a particular case, you still have two steps open to you. One is to ask your instructor, the reader you are seeking to inform in the first place. The other, if you find it impracticable to contact your teacher, is to use the footnote. Having an unnecessary footnote is a minor flaw. Not having a necessary one is a serious omission. So you can simply err on the safe side.

Now that you know when to use footnotes, you can consider the matter of how to use them. There are several commonly used formats. Simply ask your instructor which one is preferred. If your teacher has no preference, amble over to your campus bookstore and invest in the University of Chicago's *Manual of Style*. It is brief, clearly written, reliable, and cheap. It is very unlikely you will encounter a question the *Manual of Style* will not answer.

WHAT TO INCLUDE IN YOUR BIBLIOGRAPHY

Early in your research you compiled a list of possible sources. The temptation is to type out a bibliography from those cards. This is fine provided that you actually used all of those sources. Your bibliography should include all the sources you consulted and only the sources you consulted. So even though you have all sorts of cards, and even though your bibliography would look far more impressive if you included sources you looked up but did not use, do not. The game is

not worth the candle. Your instructor will have a quite accurate sense of what sources you used just from reading your paper. So it is most unlikely that padding your bibliography will impress. In fact, your teacher is more than likely to challenge your reliability if any part of your paper seems padded. In scholarship, honesty really is the best policy.

A WORD ABOUT PLAGIARISM AND ABOUT ORIGINALITY

Plagiarism is the act of claiming another's work as your own. It is about as serious an offense as you can commit. Many colleges require teachers to report all instances of plagiarism and, while the punishment can vary, it is always stiff. Moreover, of all the various ways of cheating teachers find plagiarism the easiest to detect.

Some students even manage to plagiarize without realizing that this is what they are doing. They either quote or paraphrase a book or article without indicating that. (They omit the quotation marks or they omit the footnote.) They have, without necessarily intending to, passed off someone else's work as their own. Sometimes this results in nothing worse than a private lecture from the instructor on the necessity of correctly attributing all information. Even so it is embarrassing, and it creates the impression that you do not know what you are doing. So, be sure you indicate the sources not only of your information but also of the interpretations or ideas you include in your papers.

Teachers will often tell their students that their papers should be original. Since scholars use this word in a somewhat different sense than you might expect, a word of explanation may prove helpful. In ordinary speech something is original if it is the first of its kind or if it is the only one of its kind. Historians and other scholars mean something less dramatic than that. We refer to research as "original" if the researcher did the work himself. We do not mean that his conclusions have never been reached before or that no one else has ever used his source materials. The way you put familiar information and ideas together may be original.

Do not hesitate to make use of ideas from other historians. No one with any sense expects beginning students to make startling discoveries or to develop radically new perspectives on the past. Of course it would be wonderful if you did, but no one anticipates that you will. It is, accordingly, perfectly legitimate for you to use other people's insights. The only hitch is that you must always acknowledge where they came from.

EUROPE, AFRICA, AND THE AMERICAS

SUGGESTED OUTCOMES

After studying Chapter 1, you should be able to

1. Explain the state of European knowledge in the late fifteenth century concerning the size and shape of the earth.
2. Describe European contacts with Asia in the thirteenth and fourteenth centuries and what the Europeans found attractive there.
3. Explain why Europeans became so interested in finding a water route to Asia.
4. Explain what is meant by the term "Beginnings of World History."
5. Describe the major native civilizations in the New World at the time of the arrival of the Europeans.
6. Describe political life in England on the eve of the great colonization ventures in North America.
7. Describe the various living arrangements of the Indian tribes of North America on the eve of the arrival of the English colonists.
8. Explain the meaning of the term "The Columbian Exchange."
9. Explain how the Renaissance and Reformation changed European life.
10. Explain the origins of the slave trade and why major African civilizations were unable to stop it.
11. Explain how the African climate and geography affected its historical development.

CHRONOLOGY

1415 Prince Henry of Portugal begins his explorations of the African coast.

1453 Constantinople falls to the Turks.

1485 Henry VII becomes King of England.

1487 Bartholomeu Dias of Portugal rounds the southern tip of Africa.

1492 King Ferdinand and Queen Isabella expel the last of the Moorish armies from Spain.
Columbus makes his first voyage to the New World.

1494 Spain and Portugal sign the Treaty of Tordesillas dividing the New World between them.

1497 John Cabot begins the voyage of exploration that eventually took him to Newfoundland, Labrador, and Nova Scotia and that established the British claim to North America.
Vasco da Gama of Portugal sails around the southern tip of Africa and across the Indian Ocean to India.

1509 Henry VIII begins his reign as King of England.

1513 Balboa discovers the Pacific Ocean.
Ponce de León discovers the mainland of Florida.

1519 Cortés begins his conquest of the Aztec empire in Mexico.
Ferdinand Magellan begins the voyage that will eventually circumnavigate the globe.

1524 Verrazano explores the coast of North America and establishes the French claim there.

1528 Cabeza de Vaca begins the voyage that will lead to his eight-year exploration of the northern Gulf of Mexico and then overland to the Gulf of California.

1532 Pizarro begins his conquest of the Inca empire in Peru.

1535 Cartier's explorations establish the French claim to the St. Lawrence River basin.
Spain begins its conquest of Ecuador, Chile, northern Argentina, and Bolivia.

1539 De Soto begins his exploration of the southeastern United States and reaches the Mississippi River.	**1564** France establishes the colony of Fort Caroline near present-day Jacksonville, Florida. Spanish troops destroy the colony, establishing their own settlement at St. Augustine the following year.
1540 Coronado begins his explorations of the American Southwest.	
1542 Juan Cabrillo explores the coast of California for Spain.	
1556 The staunch Catholic Philip II begins his reign as King of Spain.	**1578** Francis Drake, after attacking Spanish shipping, begins the voyage that will result in the first circumnavigation of the globe by an English ship.
1558 Elizabeth I becomes Queen of England.	
1562 John Hawkins begins his depradations against Spanish shipping.	**1588** English ships defeat the Spanish Armada.

MAP ANALYSIS

1. Carefully analyze the accompanying map and compare it with a current map of Europe, Africa, the Atlantic Ocean, and the New World. Describe the distortions in this map made in 1507.

_____

_____

_____

_____

_____

_____

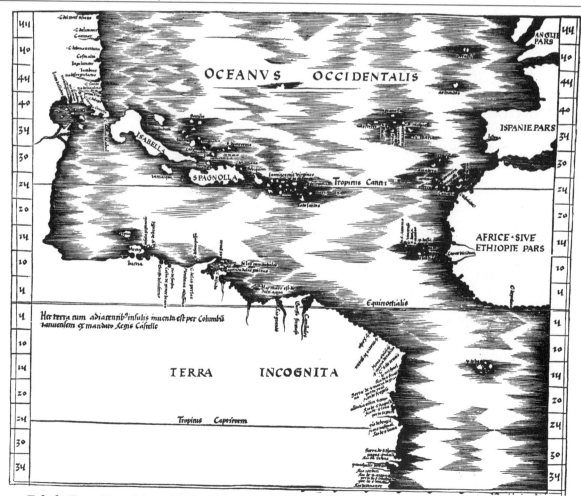

18 *Tabula Terre Nove,* **Map of the New World, 1507–1513.** *(N. Phelps Stokes Collection. Prints Division. The New York Public Library, Astor, Lenox and Tilden Foundations)*

2. Analyze the map below. Why did the increase in the power of the Ottoman Empire stimulate the desire of western Europeans to find a water route to Asia?

_____
_____
_____
_____
_____
_____
_____
_____
_____
_____
_____
_____
_____

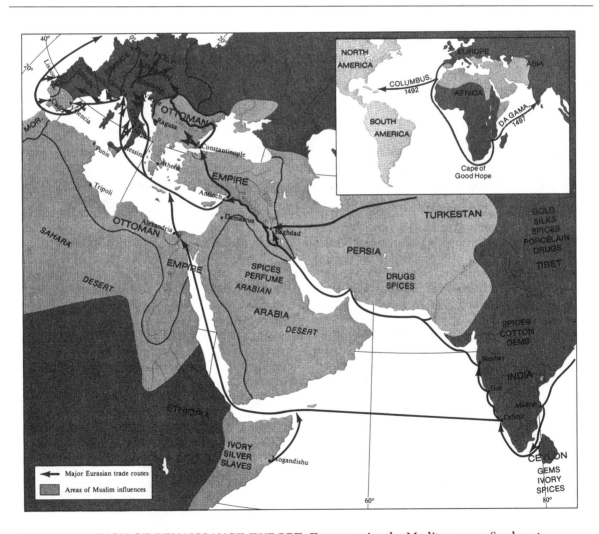

THE EXPANSION OF RENAISSANCE EUROPE. For centuries the Mediterranean Sea lay at the center of the trade routes of Europe, northern Africa, and southern Asia. Since 700 A.D., Muslim traders controlled this commerce, and Arab civilization flourished in Alexandria and Constantinople. Beginning in the 1490s, Spanish, Portuguese, and Dutch adventurers and merchants opened up new trade routes and changed the pattern of world commerce.

19

3. Look at the map below. Using the material in the textbook, compare and contrast the living arrangements of some Indian tribes living in different regions.

_____

_____

_____

_____

_____

_____

_____

_____

_____

_____

_____

_____

_____

_____

_____

_____

_____

_____

_____

_____

_____

_____

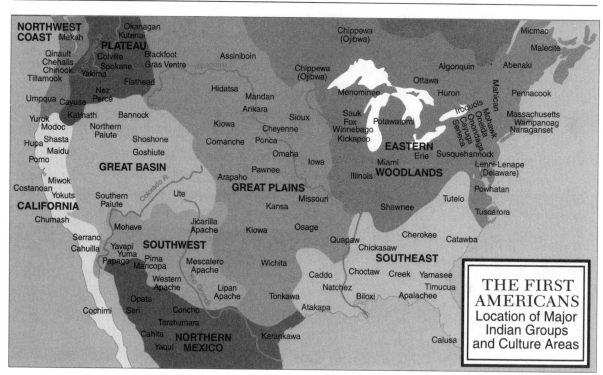

NATIVE-AMERICAN CULTURAL DIVERSITY. The Indians of eastern North America spoke four major languages—Algonquin, Muskogean, Iroquois, and Sioux. Each language group consisted of many separate tribes, ranging in size from two thousand to twenty thousand persons. The members of each tribe spoke a distinct dialect and married among themselves. Tribal rivalries and linguistic diversity often hindered united Indian resistance to the English.

PHOTOGRAPH AND ILLUSTRATION ANALYSIS

1. Look at the drawing of the Great Temple of Tenochtitlán. How do you think Cortés reacted when he first encountered the temple?

_____

_____

_____

_____

_____

_____

_____

_____

_____

_____

_____

_____

_____

_____

_____

_____

_____

_____

_____

_____

The Great Temple of Tenochtitlán reconstructed by Ignacio Marquina from descriptions by Spanish conquerors and existing Aztec monuments. *(Courtesy, American Museum of Natural History)*

2. Look at the sketch of Indian life. How did the Indians catch fish when they did not possess iron or steel fishing hooks? What unusual elements are in the sketch and how would you explain them?

_____

_____

_____

_____

_____

"They have likewise a notable way to catche fishe in their Rivers, for whear as they lack both yron, and steele, they faste unto their Reedes or longe Rodds, the hollowe tayle of a certain fishe like to a sea crabbe in steede of a poynte, wehr with by nighte or day they stricke fishes, and take them opp into their boates."—Hariot (1590). John White, *The Manner of Their Fishing*, drawing 1585. *(Courtesy, British Museum, London)*

VOCABULARY

The following words may not be part of your normal vocabulary. If their meaning is not familiar to you, you should look them up in a dictionary.

atrocious	circumnavigation	enmity	domesticate
bacillus	encroachments	confiscate	arid
hieroglyphics	decimate	plunder	kaleidescope
stalemate	tyranny	audacious	lineage
entrepôts	fiscal	nomadic	ostracism
fanaticism	annulment	egalitarian	hierarchical

22

IDENTIFICATION OF KEY CONCEPTS

In two to three sentences, identify each of the following:

The Middle Passage _____

_____

_____

_____

African Slave Trade _____

_____

_____

_____

Islam _____

_____

_____

_____

Aztecs _____

_____

_____

_____

Incas _____

_____

_____

_____

Maya _____

_____

_____

_____

Spanish Armada _____

_____

_____

_____

Iroquois_____

_____

_____

_____

Columbian Exchange _____

_____

_____

_____

IDENTIFICATION OF KEY INDIVIDUALS

In two to three sentences, identify each of the following:

Marco Polo _____

_____

_____

_____

Christopher Columbus _____

_____

_____

_____

Prince Henry _____

_____

_____

_____

Ferdinand Magellan _____

_____

_____

_____

Hernán Cortés _____

_____

_____

_____

Montezuma II _____

_____

_____

_____

Hernando de Soto _____

_____

_____

_____

Olaudah Equiano _____

_____

_____

Jacques Cartier _____

_____

_____

_____

Francisco Vásquez de Coronado _____

_____

_____

_____

NAME _____ DATE _____

Martin Luther_____
_____
_____
_____

Henry VII and Henry VIII_____
_____
_____
_____

Elizabeth I _____
_____
_____
_____

Francis Drake_____
_____
_____
_____

SELF-TEST
Multiple-Choice Questions

1. The ancestors of present-day African Americans first came to the U.S. from which African region?
   a. western
   b. northern
   c. eastern
   d. southern

2. Reasons Englishmen gave for desiring colonies in America included all of these except to
   a. relieve overpopulation.
   b. prevent Spanish expansion.
   c. enrich themselves and the kingdom.
   d. spread the Catholic religion in the New World.

3. The Aztecs
   a. were a peace-loving tribe in South America.
   b. defeated the Spanish conquistadores.
   c. held vast amounts of spices.
   d. were nearly wiped out by smallpox.

4. The Columbian Exchange refers to
   a. the ransom of Columbus by Europeans.
   b. a redistribution of plants, animals, and peoples around the globe.
   c. the purchase of Manhattan for $24.
   d. the exchange of gold for paper currency.

5. Circumstantial evidence suggests that Europeans received from native Americans
   a. horses.   c. syphillis.
   b. smallpox.   d. cats.

6. How many trips did Columbus make to the New World?
   a. one
   b. two
   c. four
   d. eight

7. Spices were more than a luxury for Europeans; they were important
   a. preservatives.
   b. for farm animals.
   c. for trade with the New World.
   d. to satisfy the barbarians.

8. The only South American country that today speaks Portuguese and was awarded to Portugal by the Treaty of Tordesillas is
   a. Nicargua.
   b. Argentina.
   c. Brazil.
   d. Chile.

9. British monarchs of the sixteenth and seventeenth centuries include all but
   a. Henry VII.
   b. Henry VIII.
   c. Elizabeth I.
   d. George III.

10. The Five Nations Confederation was a phenomenon of the
   a. Northeast.
   b. Southeast.
   c. Northwest.
   d. Southwest.

Matching Questions

For questions 11 through 15, use one of the lettered items.

11. Conqueror of the Inca Empire in Peru.___
12. Explored the West Coast of the present-day United States.___
13. Conqueror of the Aztec Empire in Mexico.___
14. Spanish explorer who first landed at Florida.___
15. Spanish explorer who discovered the Pacific Ocean.___

   a. Francisco Pizarro
   b. Hernán Cortés
   c. Ponce de León
   d. Vasco Núñez de Balboa
   e. Juan Rodriguez Cabrillo

True-False Questions

16. The hunter-gatherer Indians of North America primarily lived in the forests of the eastern regions.___
17. The so-called Mound Builders lived in the deserts of Utah and Nevada.___
18. During the sixteenth century, the native American population of the New World underwent a drastic decline.___
19. Francis Drake was the first explorer to circumnavigate the globe.___
20. Atahualpa was the leader of the Aztec Empire of Mexico.___

Essay Questions

1. Why did the Age of Discovery occur when it did? What are the similarities and differences between the Age of Discovery and our own age of space exploration?

_____

_____

_____

_____

_____

_____

_____
_____
_____
_____
_____
_____
_____
_____
_____
_____
_____
_____
_____
_____
_____
_____
_____
_____
_____
_____

2. Some historians view Indian-white relations as an inevitable "clash of cultures" and try to avoid assessing blame. Other historians argue that the "clash of cultures" approach eliminates important moral questions and serves, knowingly or not, to justify European subjugation of the Indian tribes. How would you approach the controversial question of Indian-white relations?

_____
_____
_____
_____
_____
_____
_____
_____
_____
_____
_____
_____
_____
_____
_____
_____
_____
_____
_____
_____

3. Explain how African history became strongly involved with United States history. Make some reference to events of the nineteenth and twentieth centuries.

_____

_____

_____

_____

_____

_____

_____

_____

_____

_____

_____

4. Distinguish among the Incas, Maya, and Aztecs.

_____

_____

_____

_____

_____

_____

_____

_____

_____

_____

_____

5. Did European expansion make the New Wortld a better place?

_____

_____

_____

_____

_____

_____

_____

_____

_____

_____

_____

Self-Test Answers
1. a 2. d 3. d 4. b 5. c 6. c 7. a 8. c 9. d 10. a 11. a
12. e 13. b 14. c 15. d 16. F 17. F 18. T 19. F 20. F

 **NORTH AMERICA**

SUGGESTED OUTCOMES
After studying Chapter 2, you should be able to
1. Describe the early history of the English settlements in Virginia.
2. Explain Puritan theology and describe what the Puritan groups hoped to achieve by settling in America.
3. Explain why Rhode Island was described as the "Colony of Dissidents" during its early years.
4. Describe the role of Roman Catholics in settling Maryland.
5. Describe the impact of the English Civil War on the American colonies.
6. Explain Quaker theology and why William Penn established the Pennsylvania colony.
7. Explain the meaning of the term "mercantilism" and the relationship of the Navigation Acts to mercantilism.
8. Describe the conflicts between Indians and English settlers in seventeenth-century America.
9. Explain the causes, outcome, and significance of Bacon's Rebellion in Virginia.
10. Provide the history and significance of the Dominion of New England.
11. Explain the significance of the Glorious Revolution.
12. Explain the political philosophy of John Locke.
13. Discuss the nature of religious freedom in various regions of colonial America.

CHRONOLOGY
1587 Sir Walter Raleigh founds the Roanoke Colony.

1607 Virginia Company establishes settlement at Jamestown.

1619 The House of Burgesses, a representative legislature, is established.

1620 The Mayflower Compact is signed. The Pilgrims establish the colony at Plymouth, Massachusetts.

1624 The charter of the Virginia Company is annulled and Virginia becomes a royal colony. The Dutch establish their first settlements in New Netherlands.

1625 Charles I becomes King of England.

1629 Massachusetts Bay Company is organized.

1630 Large-scale emigration of Puritans from England begins.

1634 Lord Baltimore begins the settlements in Maryland.

1635 Roger Williams is expelled from Massachusetts Bay.

1636 Harvard College is established. The first permanent English settlements are established in Rhode Island and Connecticut.

1638 Anne Hutchinson is expelled from Massachusetts Bay. New Sweden is established in present-day Delaware.

1642 The English Civil War begins, as does the period of "Salutary Neglect" of the colonies.

1643 The Confederation of New England is formed.

1644 Rhode Island receives its patent.

1649 Charles I is executed in England. Maryland passes the Toleration Act.

1660 The Stuart monarchy is restored, and Charles II becomes King of England. Parliament passes the Navigation Act of 1660.

1662 Puritan ministers implement the Half-Way Covenant in Massachusetts.

1663 Parliament passes the Staple Act of 1663.	**1681** William Penn receives the proprietary grant of Pennsylvania.
1664 England takes control of New Netherlands and renames the colony New York. New Jersey is granted to two proprietors.	**1682** The first European settlements begin in Pennsylvania.
	1686 The Dominion of New England is established.
1670 The city of Charleston in present-day South Carolina is established.	**1688** The Glorious Revolution occurs in England.
1675 King Philip's War begins in New England.	
1676 Bacon's Rebellion occurs in Virginia.	**1689** Leisler's Rebellion begins in New York.
1677 Culpepper's Rebellion occurs in Carolina.	**1696** Parliament passes the Navigation Act of 1696.
1680 New Hampshire receives a royal charter.	

PHOTOGRAPH AND ILLUSTRATION ANALYSIS

1. The illustration shows New York City (New Amsterdam) as it existed in the 1620s. Compare the settlement then with your knowledge of the city today.

_____

_____

_____

_____

_____

_____

_____

_____

_____

This 1651 engraving, the earliest known view of Manhattan Island, shows the fort of New Amsterdam in the 1620s. Indians are bringing beaver pelts in their canoes to sell to the Dutch.

MAP EXERCISE

1. Look at the map below. Why did the settlers of New England stay relatively close to the seacoast or to a major river?

_____

_____

_____

_____

_____

_____

_____

_____

_____

_____

_____

_____

_____

_____

SETTLEMENT PATTERNS IN NEW ENGLAND. By 1700, the Puritans had spread along the Atlantic Coast and far up the broad plains of the Connecticut River Valley.

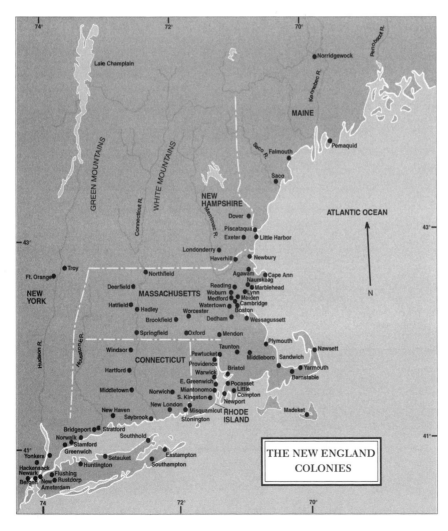

THE NEW ENGLAND COLONIES

VOCABULARY

The following words may not be part of your normal vocabulary. If their meaning is not familiar to you, you should look them up in a dictionary.

sachem	secular	royalist	papist
genocidal	dissident	intermittently	oligarchy
saline	suffrage	impediment	sovereign
succumb	clerical	demagogue	ecclesiastical
averse	feasible	devoid	encumbered
theocracy	laxity	coherence	unsavory
seditious	burgeoning	communicant	

IDENTIFICATION OF KEY CONCEPTS

In two to three sentences, identify each of the following:

Pequot War _____

_____

_____

_____

Roanoke Colony _____

_____

_____

_____

Jamestown_____

_____

_____

_____

Puritans _____

_____

_____

_____

Separatists _____

_____

_____

_____

predestination _____

_____

_____

_____

Massachusetts Bay Colony _____

_____

_____

_____

Mayflower Compact _____
_____
_____
_____

Half-Way Covenant _____
_____
_____
_____

Navigation Acts _____
_____
_____
_____

mercantilism _____
_____
_____
_____

King Philip's War _____
_____
_____
_____

Bacon's Rebellion _____
_____
_____
_____

Dominion of New England _____
_____
_____
_____

Glorious Revolution _____
_____
_____
_____

IDENTIFICATION OF KEY INDIVIDUALS

In two to three sentences, identify each of the following:

Anne Hutchinson _____
_____
_____
_____

Walter Raleigh _____

_____

_____

John Smith _____

_____

_____

John Winthrop _____

_____

_____

Roger Williams _____

_____

_____

George Calvert _____

_____

_____

William Bradford _____

_____

_____

Nathaniel Bacon _____

_____

_____

John Locke _____

_____

_____

SELF-TEST
Multiple-Choice Questions

1. The Navigation Acts passed during the 1660s primarily
    a. stimulated trade between the colonies and Spain.
    b. encouraged the immigration of slaves.
    c. regulated trade within the empire.
    d. forbade the colonies to compete against England's munitions industry.

NAME _____ DATE _____

2. Bacon's Rebellion was for the most part
   a. a result of Governor Berkeley's indifference to native American attacks on the frontier.
   b. a revolt by landless indentured servants.
   c. the Virginia planters' attempt to throw off English rule.
   d. a protest against the high cost of food.

3. A major difference between the New England colonies and the southern colonies was that
   a. the New England colonists were religious and southern colonists were not concerned with religion.
   b. southerners were interested in transplanting English political and social institutions, and New Englanders sought to establish new institutions.
   c. while settlement in New England was within ordered communities; southern settlement was widely dispersed.
   d. the New England colonies forbade indentured servitude and the southern colonies did not.

4. William Penn's *Frame of Government*
   a. required the enforcement of the Navigation Acts.
   b. provided that legislative power would be vested in a council and an assembly.
   c. gave strict control of taxation to the proprietor or his deputy.
   d. provided that none should profit from selling land.

5. Separatists formerly of the Church of England settled
   a. Boston.
   b. Jamestown.
   c. Albany.
   d. Plymouth on Cape Cod.

6. Predestination was an important tenet of early
   a. Quakers.
   b. Roman Catholics.
   c. Puritans.
   d. native Americans.

7. Among Puritans good behavior was a sign that they were among the
   a. saved "elect."
   b. non-elect.
   c. healthy of body.
   d. most intelligent.

8. The only one of the first thirteen colonies that was originally settled by Roman Catholics in significant numbers and influence was
   a. Delaware.
   b. Maryland.
   c. South Carolina.
   d. Connecticut.

9. The colony of New York, or New Amsterdam, was originally settled by
   a. Swedes.
   b. Germans.
   c. Dutch.
   d. British.

10. The Northwest Passage
    a. was the water route to the New World.
    b. was where the English defeated the Spanish Armada.
    c. was the dream of a water route to the Orient.
    d. provided safe transit for early colonists.

Matching Questions

For questions 11 through 15, use one of the lettered items.

11. Leader of the Dominion of New England.___
12. Leader of the Separatist colony at Plymouth.___
13. Leader of the Puritan settlement at Massachusetts Bay.___
14. Founder of the Roanoke colony.___
15. Leader of the Jamestown settlement.___

a. Walter Raleigh
b. John Smith
c. John Winthrop
d. William Bradford
e. Edmund Andros

For questions 16 through 20, use one of the lettered items.

16. Leader of the New England Indians.___
17. Leader of the Virginia Indians.___
18. Leader of the Quaker colonists.___
19. The dissident Puritan who helped found Rhode Island.___
20. The English philosopher.___

a. Powhatan
b. King Philip
c. William Penn
d. Roger Williams
e. John Locke

True-False Questions

21. During the years of the English Civil War, political officials in London constantly interfered in colonial affairs.___
22. Maryland and Pennsylvania were both initially settled by people escaping religious persecution in England.___
23. The primary purpose of the Navigation Acts was to implement mercantilism.___
24. The first successful, permanent colony in British North America was Roanoke.___
25. Bacon's Rebellion in Virginia was primarily inspired by conflict between colonists and Indians in the western frontier.___

Essay Questions

1. The Puritan migration to Massachusetts raises the timeless dilemma of whether dissenters should try to change the existing system from within or without. After years of trying to change England through political means, some Puritans withdrew to the New World, hoping to become an example for the rest of the world to follow. Did the Puritans succeed? Can you think of other groups in American history who have faced a similar demand?

_____

_____

_____

_____

_____

_____

_____

_____

_____

_____

_____

_____

_____

_____

_____

_____

_____

_____

_____

_____

2. What was the significance of Bacon's Rebellion? Does it reveal anything about the relationship between social and political mobility that might also have application today?

_____

_____

_____

_____

_____

_____

_____

_____

_____

_____

_____

_____

_____

_____

_____

_____

_____

_____

_____
_____
_____
_____
_____
_____
_____
_____
_____
_____
_____
_____
_____
_____
_____
_____
_____
_____
_____
_____
_____
_____
_____
_____

Self-Test Answers

1. c 2. a 3. c 4. b 5. d 6. c 7. a 8. b 9. c 10. c 11. e 12. d
13. c 14. a 15. b 16. b 17. a 18. c 19. d 20. e 21. F
22. T 23. T 24. F 25. T

THE DEVELOPING COLONIES

SUGGESTED OUTCOMES

After studying Chapter 3, you should be able to
1. Explain the origins and significance of the Salem witchcraft controversy.
2. Describe daily life in colonial New England and the nature of its economy.
3. Describe the German minority group in early America.
4. Describe the Scotch-Irish minority group in early America.
5. Compare and contrast Indian-white relations in the Middle colonies with those in the Southern colonies.
6. Describe how Quaker values affected life in Pennsylvania.
7. Describe the evolution of slavery in early America.
8. Discuss the founding of Georgia and the Carolinas.
9. Describe the origins and significance of the Great Awakening.
10. Describe the status of American women during the colonial period.
11. Give a brief ethnic portrait of America as it existed in 1750.
12. Explain the relationship between empiricism and the Enlightenment.
13. Explain why colonial America was more democratic than England.
14. Describe the effectiveness of the British imperial system as it existed in 1750.

CHRONOLOGY

1662 Puritan ministers implement the Half-Way Covenant in Massachusetts.
The House of Burgesses in Virginia declares lifetime servitude for African servants.
1676 Bacon's Rebellion occurs in Virginia.
1691 College of William and Mary is established.
1692 The witchcraft controversy begins in Salem, Massachusetts.
1699 Parliament passes the Wool Act.
1701 Yale College is established.
1711 Tuscarora Rebellion begins in North Carolina.
1712 Slave rebellion occurs in New York City.
1715 Yamasee Rebellion begins in South Carolina.
1732 Parliament passes the Hat Act.
1733 The Georgia colony is established.
Parliament passes the Sugar Act.
1734 The Great Awakening begins in colonial America.

1735 The trial of John Peter Zenger occurs in New York.
1743 The American Philosophical Society is founded in Philadelphia.
1750 Parliament passes the Iron Act.

PHOTOGRAPH AND ILLUSTRATION ANALYSIS

1. Analyze the sketch below. How does it illustrate the arguments made by Great Awakening preachers?

_____

_____

_____

_____

_____

_____

George Whitefield and John Wesley promised salvation to those who opened their hearts to God through prayer. To them was offered eternal life in the New Jerusalem depicted in this drawing; to others the door to Hell stood open. *(Courtesy, Scribner's Archives)*

DOCUMENTS ANALYSIS

1. Read the advertisements reprinted on the next page. What can you conclude about the living arrangements of indentured servants?

_____

_____

_____

_____

_____

_____

Philadelphia, April 14, 1748.

Run away from Samuel Lippincott of Northampton in the county of Burlington, an Irish servant Maid, named Mary Muckleroy, of a middle Stature: Had on when she went away, a blue and white striped gown, of large and small stripes, cuffed with blue, a white muslin handkerchief, an old blue quilt, a new Persian black bonnet, a new pair of calf-skin shoes, a fine Holland cap, with a cambrick border, an old black short cloak lined with Bengal, blue worsted stockings, with white clocks, a very good fine shirt, and a very good white apron. She took with her a sorrel horse, about 14 hands high, shod before, and paces very well. It is supposed there is an Irishman gone with her. Whoever takes up and secures the said woman and horse, so that they may be had again, shall have Three Pounds reward, and reasonable charges paid by

Samuel Lippincott
—*The Pennsylvania Gazette, April 16, 1748. . . .*

Philadelphia, June 8. 1749.

Run away from *Nicholas Bearcraft* of *Hunterdon County,* a Black Wench, named *Hecatissa* alias *Savina,* Country born, about 27 Years of Age, short Stature, gloomy down Look, often troubl'd with the Cholick, it is thought she may be gone towards Maryland. Whoever takes up and secures said Wench, so that she may be had again, shall have *Twenty Shillings* Reward, and reasonable Charges, paid by

NICHOLAS BEARCRAFT.
—*The Pennsylvania Journal, June 8, 1749. . . .*

2. In what ways does the following sermon illustrate the values and cultural atmosphere of the Great Awakening? How did Nathan Cole react to the sermon by the Reverend George Whitefield?

_____
_____
_____
_____
_____
_____
_____
_____
_____
_____
_____
_____
_____
_____
_____
_____
_____
_____

SINNERS IN THE HANDS OF AN ANGRY GOD *by Jonathan Edwards.*

Among the preachers associated with the Great Awakening, Edwards is the most famous. His sermons embodied the tremendous emotionalism of a powerful religious revival.

The God that holds you over the pit of hell, much as one holds a spider, or some loathsome insect, over the fire, abhors you, and you, and is dreadfully provoked; his wrath towards you burns like fire; he looks upon you as worthy of nothing else, but to be cast into the fire; he is of purer eyes than to bear to have you in his sight; you are ten thousand times so abominable in his eyes, as the most hateful and venomous serpent is in ours. You have offended him infinitely more than ever a stubborn rebel did his prince: and yet it is nothing but his hand that holds you from falling into the fire every moment: it is ascribed to nothing else, that you did not go to hell the last night; that you was suffered to awake again in this world, after you closed your eyes to sleep; and there is no other reason to be given, why you have not dropped into hell since you arose in the morning, but that God's hand has held you up: there is no other reason to be given why you have not gone to hell, since you have sat here in the house of God, provoking his pure eyes by your sinful wicked manner of attending his solemn worship: yea, there is nothing else that is to be given as a reason why you do not this very moment drop down into hell. . . .

How dreadful is the state of those that are daily and hourly in danger of this great wrath and infinite misery! But this is the dismal case of every soul in this congregation that has not been born again, however moral and strict, sober and religious, they may otherwise be. . . . There is reason to think, that there are many in this congregation now hearing this discourse, that will actually be the subjects of this very misery to all eternity. We know not who they are, or in what seats they sit, or what thoughts they now have. . . . It would be no wonder if some persons, that now sit here in some seats of this meeting-house in health, and quiet and secure, should be there in hell before tomorrow morning.

NATHAN COLE, *a farmer and carpenter of Connecticut, breathlessly anticipated George Whitefield's great sermon.*

There came a messenger and said Mr. Whitfield preached at Hartford and Weathersfield yesterday and is to preach at Middeltown this morning at 10 o clock. I was in my field at work [and] I dropt my tool that I had in my hand and run home and run thru my house and bade my wife get ready quick to goo and hear Mr. Whitfield preach at Middeltown. And [I] run to my pasture for my hors with all my might, fearing I should be too late to hear him. I brought my hors home and soon mounted and took my wife up and went forward as fast as I thought my hors could bear, and when my hors began to be out of breath I would get down and put my wife on the Saddel, and bid her ride as fast as she could, and not Stop or Slak for except I bade her. And so I would run until I was almost out of breth, and then mount my hors again, and so I did severel times to favour my hors. . . .

When we came within about half a mile of the road that comes down from Hartford, Weathersfield and Stepney to Middeltown, on high land, I saw before me a Cloud or fog, rising—I first thought—off from the great river. But as I came nearer the road I heard a noise, something like a low rumbling thunder, and I presently found it was the rumbling of horses feet coming down the road and this Cloud was a Cloud of dust made by the running of horses feet. It arose some rods into the air over the tops of the hills and trees. And when I came within about twenty rods of the road, I could see men and horses Slipping along in the Cloud like shadows. And when I came nearer it was like a stedy streem of horses and their riders, scarcely a horse more than his length behind another, all of a lather and fome with swet, ther breth rooling out of their noistrels. . . . Every hors semed to go with all his might to carry his rider to hear the news from heaven for the saving of their Souls. It made me trembel to see the Sight.

We went down in the Streeme. I herd no man speak a word all the way, three mile, but evry one presing forward in great haste. And when we gat down to the old meating house, thare was a great multitude. It was said to be 3 or 4000 of people assembled together.

We gat of from our horses and shook off the dust, and the ministers was then coming to the meating house. I turned and looked toward the great river and saw the fery boats running swift forward and backward, bringing over loads of people. The ores rowed nimble and quick. Everything—men, horses and boats—all seamed to be struglin for life. The land and the banks over the river looked black with people and horses all along the 12 miles. I see no man at work in his field, but all seamed to be gone.

When I see Mr. Whitfield come upon the Scaffold, he looked almost angellical—a young, slim, slender youth before some thousands of people, and with a bold, undaunted countenance. And my hearing how God was with him everywhere as he came along, it solomnized my mind, and put me in a trembling fear before he began to preach, for he looked as if he was Cloathed with authority from the great God.

3. Read the accompanying poem. What was "bundling?" How successful do you think it was as a means of providing privacy but not sexual intimacy to an unmarried couple?

_____

_____

_____

_____

_____

_____

_____

_____

_____

_____

_____

_____

_____

BUNDLING

Courting couples had little privacy to hug and kiss. A sensible solution, to these sensible people, was to take the beloved under the covers. The results were unpredictable, as this nineteenth-century poem suggests.

Whether they must be hugg'd or Kiss'd when sitting by the fire
Or whether they in bed may lay, which doth the Lord require?
In Genesis no knowledge is of this thing to be got,
Whether young men did bundle then, or whether they did not.
The sacred book says wives they took, it don't say how they courted.
Whether that they in bed did lay, or by the fire sported.

Young miss, if this your habit be, I'll teach you now yourself to see:
You plead you're honest, modest too, but such a plea will never do;
For how can modesty consist, with shameful practice such as this?
I'll give your answer to the life: You don't undress, like man and wife.
That is your plea, I'll freely own, but who's your bondsman when alone,
That further rules you will not break, and marriage liberties partake?
But you will say that I'm unfair, that some who bundle take more care,
For some we may in truth suppose, bundle in bed with all their clothes.
But bundler's clothes are no defense, unruly horses push the fence.

VOCABULARY

The following words may not be part of your normal vocabulary. If their meaning is not familiar to you, you should look them up in a dictionary.

demoniac	paupers	empiricism	manumission
liaison	slovenly	presumptous	recalcitrant
aristocracy	inexorable	indigo	pedagogical
maritime	denizens	gender	expediency
entrepreneurs	rectitude	insubordination	elite
polity	charismatic	mulatto	

IDENTIFICATION OF KEY CONCEPTS

In two to three sentences, identify each of the following:

Salem witchcraft controversy _____

_____

_____

_____

Scotch-Irish_____

_____

_____

William Penn and the Indians _____

_____

_____

_____

Quakers _____

_____

_____

_____

Indians in the Southern Colonies _____

_____

_____

_____

Tuscarora Rebellion _____

_____

_____

_____

Yamasee Rebellion _____

_____

_____

_____

Colonial slavery_____

_____

_____

_____

Virginia social structure _____

_____

_____

_____

Great Awakening _____

_____

_____

_____

Enlightenment _____
_____
_____
_____

Colonial women _____
_____
_____
_____

legal status of colonial women _____
_____
_____
_____

indentured servitude _____
_____
_____
_____

theories of aristocracy and democracy_____
_____
_____
_____

empiricism _____
_____
_____
_____

town vs. country divisions_____
_____
_____
_____

impact of the labor shortage on colonial economic life _____
_____
_____
_____

IDENTIFICATION OF KEY INDIVIDUALS

In two to three sentences, identify each of the following:

Cotton Mather _____
_____
_____
_____

William Penn _____

_____

_____

James Oglethorpe _____

_____

_____

Jonathan Edwards_____

_____

_____

George Whitefield _____

_____

_____

Benjamin Franklin _____

_____

_____

John Peter Zenger _____

_____

_____

_____

SELF-TEST

Multiple-Choice Questions

1. The Salem witchcraft episode occurred in the
   a. 1650s.
   b. 1660s.
   c. 1680s.
   d. 1690s.

2. Important colonial exports included all but
   a. tobacco.
   b. lumber.
   c. rice.
   d. horses.

3. Which statement about seventeenth-century New England is false?
   a. Most farmers lived in villages.
   b. Most of the population attended church.
   c. Great value was placed on higher education.
   d. Most people dressed in gray or black.

4. Quakerism is most closely identified with the colony of
   a. Massachusetts.
   b. New York.
   c. Pennsylvania.
   d. Virginia.

5. The growth of slavery in late seventeenth-century Virginia was encouraged by all but
   a. high tobacco prices.
   b. low tobacco prices.
   c. the high cost of white labor.
   d. the familiarity of Africans with agriculture.

6. African slaves taught southern colonists how to
   a. raise rice.
   b. raise guinea corn.
   c. fish.
   d. All of the above.

7. One of the few groups regularly to denounce slavery was the
   a. Puritans.
   b. Quakers.
   c. Anabaptists.
   d. native Americans.

8. Which phenomenon is most opposed to the spirit of the Great Awakening?
   a. the Enlightenment
   b. revivalism
   c. the lazy South
   d. antinomianism

9. The theory that nations should increase their wealth, measured in gold, by policies that ensure they will sell more than they import is known as
   a. monetarism.
   b. mercantilism.
   c. laissez-faire.
   d. democracy.

10. The Scotch-Irish settled chiefly in
    a. western Pennsylvania.
    b. tidewater Virginia.
    c. Maryland.
    d. Vermont.

11. The British government was
    a. quite democratic.
    b. divided into three parts or bodies.
    c. thoroughly aristocratic.
    d. lacking an aristocratic body.

12. Two great American revivalist preachers were
    a. John Winthrop and Anne Hutchinson.
    b. William Penn and James Oglethorpe.
    c. Jonathan Edwards and George Whitefield.
    d. Anne Bradstreet and Roger Williams.

13. The colony of Georgia had a common boundary with
    a. Virginia.
    b. South Carolina.
    c. Texas.
    d. North Carolina.

14. In 1750, African Americans constituted what percent of the colonial population.

    a. 60   b. 40   c. 20   d. 10

15. The first college established in British North America was
    a. Harvard.
    b. Columbia.
    c. Yale.
    d. William and Mary.

Matching Questions

For questions 16 through 20, use one of the lettered tems.

16. The founder of the Pennsylvania colony.___
17. The American-born preacher who played a key role in the Great Awakening.___
18. The most famous preacher of the Great Awakening.___
19. The founder of the Georgia colony.___
20. The New York newspaper publisher who argued that truth is a legal defense against libel.___

a. James Oglethorpe
b. John Peter Zenger
c. Jonathan Edwards
d. George Whitefield
e. William Penn

True-False Questions

21. Only when they married did colonial women secure the right to own property.___
22. The major American port in the mid-eighteenth century was Philadelphia.___
23. German redemptioners settled primarily in Georgia.___
24. In the colonies voting was more widespread than in England.___
25. The Great Awakening was primarily a phenomenon of New England.___

Essay Questions

1. Compare and contrast the structure of government in England with the structure of government in the individual colonies.

_____
_____
_____
_____
_____
_____

2. Characterize social mobility in the American colonies for the original settlers, for later white immigrants, for indentured servants, for blacks. How does the colonial social structure and social mobility compare with that of today?

_____
_____
_____
_____
_____
_____
_____
_____
_____
_____
_____
_____
_____
_____
_____
_____
_____
_____
_____
_____
_____
_____
_____
_____
_____
_____
_____
_____
_____
_____

3. During the Great Awakening, colonial religion split into "Old Lights" and "New Lights." What did each stand for? Does a similar split still exist in some religious groups today?

_____

_____

_____

_____

_____

_____

_____

_____

_____

_____

_____

_____

_____

_____

_____

_____

_____

_____

_____

_____

_____

_____

_____

_____

_____

_____

_____

_____

_____

Self-Test Answers

1. d 2. d 3. d 4. c 5. b 6. d 7. b 8. a 9. b 10. a 11. b 12. c
13. b 14. c 15. a 16. e 17. c 18. d 19. a 20. b 21. F 22. T
23. F 24. T 25. T

AN INDEPENDENT SPIRIT
1763–1776

SUGGESTED OUTCOMES
After studying Chapter 4, you should be able to
1. Explain why the French and Indian War led to the British decision to raise taxes in America.
2. Describe the reasons why Great Britain defeated France in the French and Indian War.
3. Explain why Great Britain ended the period of "Salutary Neglect."
4. Explain why some historians consider the Stamp Act crisis the first event of the American Revolution.
5. Explain the reasons why so many Americans opposed the Stamp Act.
6. Describe the Stamp Act Congress and explain its significance.
7. Explain why colonists hated the Quartering Act.
8. Describe the colonial use of the trade boycott against the British and determine its success.
9. Describe the Boston Massacre from the perspective of the American colonists and from the perspective of British troops.
10. Describe the evolution of the American decision to separate from Great Britain.
11. Describe the main arguments of the Declaration of Independence and how they related to the idea of individual rights.

CHRONOLOGY
1754 The Albany Plan of Union is proposed.

1756 The French and Indian War begins.

1763 The French and Indian War ends with the Treaty of Paris.
Pontiac's Rebellion erupts in the Ohio Valley.
Great Britain declares the Proclamation of 1763.
The Paxton Boys uprising occurs in Pennsylvania.

1764 Parliament passes the Sugar Act and the Currency Act.

1765 Parliament passes the Stamp Act.
The Stamp Act Congress convenes and imposes a boycott.
Sons of Liberty violently protest the Stamp Act.
Parliament passes the Quartering Act.

1766 Parliament repeals the Stamp Act and passes the Declaratory Act.

1767 Parliament passes the Townshend Duties.
Parliament establishes an American Board of Customs.

1768 John Dickinson writes "Letters of a Pennsylvania Farmer."
British troops are stationed in Boston.

1770 Lord North's ministry repeals the Townshend Duties, except the one on tea.
Boston Massacre occurs.

1772 The British schooner *Gaspée* is burned off the coast of Rhode Island.
The Boston Committee of Correspondence is established.

1773 Parliament passes the Tea Act.
The Boston Tea Party occurs.

1774 Parliament passes the Coercive (Intolerable) Acts.
First Continental Congress meets in Philadelphia.

1775 The battles of Lexington, Concord, and Bunker Hill are fought.
American forces seize Fort Ticonderoga.

The Second Continental Congress meets in Philadelphia and adopts the "Declaration of the Causes and Necessities of Taking Up Arms." George Washington is appointed commander of the Continental Army.

1776 Thomas Paine writes *Common Sense*. The Second Continental Congress issues the Declaration of Independence.

PHOTOGRAPH AND ILLUSTRATION ANALYSIS

1. Look at the sketch below. Describe what is being portrayed in the sketch.

_____

_____

_____

_____

_____

_____

_____

_____

_____

Demonstrations erupted throughout the colonies in response to "taxation without representation." In New England, suspected supporters of the hated Stamp Act were hanged in effigy.
(Courtesy, Scribner's Archives)

2. Analyze the following sketch. In what ways does it take an anti-British interpretation of the Boston Massacre?

_____

_____

_____

_____

_____

_____

The BLOODY MASSACRE perpetrated in King—Street BOSTON on March 5ᵗʰ 1770 by a party of the 29ᵗʰ REG.

" 'The Bloody Massacre perpetrated in King Street, Boston on March 5th, 1770, by a party of the 29th Reg [iment].' Engrav'd, Printed and Sold by Paul Revere, Boston."

DOCUMENTS ANALYSIS

1. Read the letters from John Andrews. How did he perceive the Boston Tea Party? Is he excited about the event? Does he express notes of disapproval? Is there any evidence of early American nationalism?

_____
_____
_____
_____
_____
_____

BOSTONIAN JOHN ANDREWS *described the tea controversy in a series of letters to his brother:*

November 29th [1773]. Hall and Bruce arriv'd Saturday evening with each an hundred and odd chests of the detested Tea. What will be done with it, can't say: but I tremble for yᵉ consequences should yᵉ consignees still persist in their obstinacy and not consent to reship it. They have softened down so far as to offer it to the care of Council or the town, till such times as they hear from their friends in England, but am perswaded, from the present dispositions of yᵉ people, that no other alternative will do, than to have it immediately sent back to London again. . . . Yᵉ bells are ringing for a general muster, and a third vessel is now arriv'd in Nantasket road. Handbills are stuck up, calling upon Friends! Citizens! and Countrymen!

December 1st. Having just return'd from Fire Club, and am now, in company with the two Miss Masons and Mr. Williams of your place, at Sam. Eliot's, who has been dining with him at Col° Hancock's, and acquaints me that Mr. Palfrey sets off Express for New York and Philadelphia at five o'clock tomorrow morning, to communicate ye transactions of this town respecting the tea. . . . The consignees have all taken their residence at the Castle, as they still persist in their refusal to take the tea back. Its not only ye town, but the country are unanimous against the landing it, and at the Monday and Tuesday Meetings, they attended to the number of some hundreds from all the neighboring towns within a dozen miles. . . .

December 18th. However precarious our situation may be, yet *such* is the present calm composure of the people that a stranger would hardly think that ten thousand pounds sterling of the East Indian Company's *tea* was destroy'd the night, or rather evening before last, yet its a serious truth; The affair was transacted with the greatest regularity and despatch. . . . A general muster was assembled, from this and all ye neighbouring towns, to the number of five or six thousand, at 10 o'clock Thursday morning in the Old South Meeting house, where they pass'd a *unanimous* vote that the *Tea* should go out of the *harbour* that afternoon, and sent a committee with Mr. Rotch to ye Custom house to *demand* a clearance, which the collector told 'em was not in his power to give, without the duties being first paid. They then sent Mr. Rotch to Milton, to ask a pass from ye Governor, who sent for answer, that "consistent with the rules of government and his duty to the King he could not grant one without they produc'd a previous clearance from the office."—By the time he return'd with this message the candles were light in [the] house, and upon reading it, such prodigious shouts were made, that induc'd me, while drinking tea at home, to go out and know the cause of it. The house was so crouded I could get no farther than ye porch, when I found the moderator was just declaring the meeting to be *dissolv'd,* which caused another general shout, out doors and in, and three cheers. What with that, and the consequent noise of breaking up the meeting, you'd thought that the inhabitants of the infernal regions had broke loose. For my part, I went contentedly home and finish'd my tea, but was soon inform'd what was going forward: but still not crediting it without ocular demonstration, I went and was *satisfied.* They muster'd, I'm told, upon Fort Hill, to the number of about two hundred, and proceeded, two by two, to Griffin's wharf, where Hall, Bruce, and Coffin lay, each with 114 chests of the *ill fated* article on board; the two former with *only* that article, but ye latter arriv'd at ye wharf only ye day before, was freighted with a large quantity of other goods, which they took the *greatest* care not to injure in the least, and before *nine* o'clock in ye evening, every chest from on board the three vessels was knock'd to pieces and flung over ye sides. They say the actors were *Indians* from *Narragansett.* Whether they were or not, to a transient observer they appear'd as *such,* being cloath'd in Blankets with the heads muffled, and copper color'd countenances, being each arm'd with a hatchet or axe, and pair pistols, nor was their *dialect* different from what I conceive these geniusses to *speak,* as their jargon was unintelligible to all but themselves.

---

2. Read the selection from Thomas Paine's *Common Sense.* What was was his main argument?

_____
_____
_____
_____
_____

COMMON SENSE *by Tom Paine*
Paine's rousing pamphlet circulated by the tens of thousands and galvanized sentiment against England in the spring of 1776.

The sun never shined on a cause of greater worth. 'Tis not the affair of a city, a county, a province, or a kingdom; but of a continent—of at least one-eighth part of the habitable globe. 'Tis not the concern of a day, a year, or an age; posterity are virtually involved in the contest, and will be more or less affected even to the end of time by the proceedings now. Now is the seedtime of continental union, faith, and honor. The least fracture now will be like a name engraved with the point of a pin on the tender rind of a young oak; the wound would enlarge with the tree, and posterity read it in full grown characters. . . .

Small islands not capable of protecting themselves are the proper objects for government to take under their care; but there is something absurd in supposing a continent to be perpetually governed by an island. In no instance hath nature made the satellite larger than its primary planet; and as England and America, with respect to each other, reverse the common order of nature, it is evident that they belong to different systems. England to Europe: America to itself. . . .

O ye that love mankind! Ye that dare oppose not only the tyranny but the tyrant, stand forth! Every spot of the old world is overrun with oppression. Freedom hath been hunted round the globe. Asia and Africa have long expelled her. Europe regards her like a stranger, and England hath given her warning to depart. O receive the fugitive, and prepare in time an asylum for mankind.

---

3. Read the newspaper article reprinted here. What does William Bradford say about the Stamp Act?

_____

_____

_____

_____

The TIMES are **Dreadful, Dismal Doleful Dolorous, and DOLLAR-LESS.**

An Emblem of the Effects of the STAMP

O! the fatal Stamp

Adieu Adieu to the LIBERTY of the PRESS

Thursday, *October* 31, 1765.   T H E   NUMB. 1195.

P E N N S Y L V A N I A   J O U R N A L ;

A N D

W E E K L Y   A D V E R T I S E R.

EXPIRING: In Hopes of a Resurrection to LIFE again.

I AM sorry to be obliged to acquaint my Readers, that as The STAMP-ACT, is fear'd to be obligatory upon us after the *First of November* ensuing, (the *fatal To-morrow*) the Publisher of this Paper unable to bear the Burthen, has thought it expedient to STOP a while, in order to deliberate, whether any Methods can be found to elude the Chains forged for us, and escape the insupportable Slavery; which it is hoped, from the last Representations now made against that Act, may be effected. Mean while, I must earnestly Request every Individual of my Subscribers. many of whom have been long behind Hand, that they would immediately Discharge their respective Arrears that I may be able, not only to support myself during the Interval, but be better prepared to proceed again with this Paper, whenever an opening for that Purpose appears, which I hope will be soon   WILLIAM BRADFORD.

Reaction to the Stamp Act by the *Pennsylvania Journal:* "The Times are Dreadful, Dismal Doleful Dolorous, and Dollar-less."

VOCABULARY

The following words may not be part of your normal vocabulary. If their meaning is not familiar to you, you should look them up in a dictionary.

bourgeois	abortive	lexicographer	boycott
censure	absolutism	subterfuge	eloquent
irony	clericalism	adamant	reconciliation
skirmish	condescension	rescind	egalitarian
premonition	indulgence	usurpers	
jeopardize	effigy	beleaguer	

IDENTIFICATION OF KEY CONCEPTS

In two to three sentences, identify each of the following:

French and Indian War _____
_____
_____
_____

Albany Plan of Union _____
_____
_____
_____

Treaty of 1763 _____
_____
_____
_____

"Salutary Neglect" _____
_____
_____
_____

Proclamation of 1763 _____
_____
_____
_____

Currency Act of 1764 _____
_____
_____
_____

Paxton Boys _____
_____
_____
_____

Revenue Act (Sugar Act) of 1764 _____
_____
_____
_____

Stamp Act of 1765 _____
_____
_____
_____

Stamp Act Congress _____
_____
_____
_____

Sons of Liberty _____
_____
_____
_____

Whig Philosophy _____
_____
_____
_____

Quartering Act of 1765 _____
_____
_____
_____

Townshend Acts of 1767 _____
_____
_____
_____

Boston Massacre _____
_____
_____
_____

"Lobsterbacks" _____
_____
_____
_____

Gaspée Affair _____
_____
_____
_____

East India Company _____
_____
_____

Boston Tea Party _____
_____
_____

Coercive (Intolerable) Acts _____
_____
_____

First Continental Congress _____
_____
_____

Battles of Lexington, Concord, and "Bunker Hill" _____
_____
_____

Loyalists _____
_____
_____

Common Sense _____
_____
_____

Declaration of Independence _____
_____
_____
_____

IDENTIFICATION OF KEY INDIVIDUALS

In two to three sentences, identify each of the following:

James Wolfe _____
_____
_____

Louis de Montcalm _____
_____
_____
_____

Edward Braddock_____
_____
_____
_____

George Grenville _____
_____
_____
_____

Charles Townsend _____
_____
_____
_____

Patrick Henry _____
_____
_____
_____

Thomas Hutchinson _____
_____
_____
_____

John Hancock_____
_____
_____
_____

George Washington _____
_____
_____
_____

Lord North _____
_____
_____
_____

John Adams_____
_____
_____
_____

Samuel Adams _____

_____

_____

_____

Phillis Wheatley _____

_____

_____

_____

Thomas Gage _____

_____

_____

Thomas Paine _____

_____

_____

_____

SELF-TEST

Multiple-Choice Questions

1. The Treaty of Paris, ending the French and Indian War, contributed to the eventual independence of the colonies by
   a. teaching Americans they could do without British products.
   b. removing the French threat to the north and west.
   c. demonstrating beyond a doubt the superiority of American militiamen to British regulars.
   d. stimulating creation of an American union centered in Albany.

2. Most effective in winning repeal of the Stamp Act was the
   a. formation of the Sons of Liberty.
   b. declaration issued by the Stamp Act Congress.
   c. work of Thomas Paine.
   d. nonimportation agreements among American businessmen.

3. All of these were effects of the Boston Tea Party except
   a. the closing of the port of Boston.
   b. the Intolerable Acts.
   c. calls for a continental congress.
   d. the confiscation of the property of known radicals.

4. One reason for British taxation measures after 1763 was
   a. the desire that colonials bear a greater share of their own administrative and defense costs.
   b. a British ministerial conspiracy.
   c. the desire to maneuver colonials into seeking representation in Parliament.
   d. the desire to make colonials pay the costs of Britain's government.

5. The Stamp Act Congress convened to
   a. declare a trade war on England.
   b. demonstrate united colonial opposition to the Stamp Tax.
   c. demand importation quotas on sugar.
   d. protest, in particular, British control of the tobacco industry.

6. The Albany Plan of Union
   a. proposed that the King appoint a president-general.
   b. was an early antifederalist document.
   c. was proposed by Britain's Parliament.
   d. was passed by a special colonial congress.

7. The Boston Massacre arose over
   a. the presence of British troops in Boston.
   b. a boundary dispute.
   c. a ship sunk in Boston Harbor.
   d. a campaign led by George Washington.

8. In the American colonies the East India Company tried to sell
   a. land grants.   c. horses.
   b. ships.   d. tea.

9. The final decision for independence
   a. represented the wishes of a sizable majority of colonists.
   b. was passed by the electorate in nine colonies.
   c. met with a good deal of opposition and indifference.
   d. was supported by the Tories.

10. The Quebec Act was unpopular because it
    a. was thought to benefit Catholics.
    b. awarded rights to the Spanish.
    c. limited Canada's boundaries.
    d. ended the French and Indian War.

Matching Questions

For questions 11 through 15, use one of the lettered items.

11. An early attempt to unify the colonies for common defense.___
12. British legislation that inspired violent resistance in America.___
13. Prohibited American settlement west of the Appalachian Mountains.___
14. Greatly extended Canadian territory and recognized Roman Catholicism.___
15. Places tariffs on glass, lead, paint, and tea.___

a. Proclamation of 1763
b. Stamp Act
c. Albany Plan
d. Townshend Duties
e. Quebec Act

For questions 16 through 20, use one of the lettered items.

16. Author of *Letters from a Pennsylvania Farmer*.___
17. Primary author of the Declaration of Independence.___
18. Author of *Common Sense*.___
19. The Chancellor of the Exchequer in England.___
20. Founder of the first public library in America.___

a. Thomas Jefferson
b. Benjamin Franklin
c. Thomas Paine
d. George Grenville
e. John Dickinson

True-False Questions

21. The Intolerable Acts closed the port of Boston and took from the colonial legislature of Massachusetts the right to appoint many colonial officials.___
22. Patrick Henry was the Boston attorney who defended the British soldiers involved in the Boston Massacre.___
23. The ship *Gaspée* was sunk by the British because it was engaged in smuggling.___
24. The Boston merchant and later patriot leader who had his ship *Liberty* seized for smuggling was John Hancock.___
25. The First Continental Congress met in response to the Sugar Act.___

Essay Questions

1. Was the American Revolution a radical or a conservative movement? Which groups benefited from the Revolution and which did not? Give at least five examples to support your answer.

_____
_____
_____
_____
_____
_____
_____
_____
_____
_____
_____
_____
_____
_____
_____
_____
_____
_____
_____
_____
_____
_____
_____
_____

_____
_____
_____
_____
_____
_____
_____
_____

2. Had you been assigned to write an article in favor of the "patriot" movement of 1776, what arguments would you have used? What issues might you avoid?

_____
_____
_____
_____
_____
_____
_____
_____
_____
_____
_____
_____
_____
_____
_____
_____
_____
_____
_____
_____
_____
_____
_____
_____
_____
_____
_____

3. Had you been asked in 1776 to create a justification for the loyalist or Tory cause, what would you have written?

_____

_____

_____

_____

_____

_____

_____

_____

_____

_____

_____

_____

_____

_____

_____

_____

_____

_____

_____

_____

_____

_____

_____

Self-Test Answers

1. b 2. d 3. d 4. a 5. b 6. a 7. a 8. d 9. c 10. a 11. c 12. b
13. a 14. e 15. d 16. e 17. a 18. c 19. d 20. b 21. T 22. F
23. F 24. T 25. F

REVOLUTION AND INDEPENDENCE 1776–1787

SUGGESTED OUTCOMES

After studying Chapter 5, you should be able to
1. Explain the significance of the Battle of Saratoga.
2. Describe the differences between the army of Great Britain and the colonial army.
3. Explain why George Washington adopted a passive strategy and why it frustrated the British. Why did the stalemate that had developed by 1779 work to the advantage of the colonists?
4. Explain what happened at the Battle of Yorktown and why it was important for the American colonies.
5. Describe the provisions of the Treaty of Paris of 1783.
6. Describe the impact of the War for American Independence on the American economy.
7. Explain how the American Revolution and the War for Independence affected land ownership, slavery, religion, Indian relations, and the status of women.
8. Describe the weaknesses inherent in the Articles of Confederation government.
9. Describe how the new American government handled the land and settlement question.
10. Explain why there was a need to convene the Constitutional Convention.
11. Discuss whether the American Revolution was really revolutionary.

CHRONOLOGY

1776 The Second Continental Congress issues the Declaration of Independence.
Battle of Trenton takes place.
Battle of Long Island takes place.
1777 Battle of Princeton occurs.
Battle of Monmouth takes place.
Battle of Brandywine Creek takes place.
Battle of Germantown occurs.
General Burgoyne surrenders at the Battle of Saratoga.
Second Continental Congress adopts the Articles of Confederation.
George Washington's troops retire to Valley Forge.
1778 United States establishes a military alliance and commercial treaty with France.
1779 Spain declares war on Great Britain.
George Rogers Clark leads an American victory in the Battle of Vincennes.
1781 Battle of Cowpens, South Carolina, takes place.

Battle of Guilford Courthouse, North Carolina, takes place.
General Cornwallis surrenders to Washington in the Battle of Yorktown.
Congress ratifies the Articles of Confederation.
1782 The Lord North ministry falls in Great Britain.
1783 The Treaty of Paris ends the War for American Independence.
1784 The Treaty of Fort Stanwix is negotiated.
1785 Congress passes the Land Ordinance of 1785.
Barbary Pirates begin harassing American shipping.
1786 Congress rejects the Jay-Gardoqui Treaty.
Annapolis Convention meets.
1787 Congress passes the Northwest Ordinance.
1795 Indians sign the Treaty of Greenville.

PHOTOGRAPH ANALYSIS

1. Look at the painting of Washington crossing the Delaware. What are some historical inaccuracies in the painting? What great event inspired the painting? What seems unrealistic about the painting?

_____

_____

_____

_____

_____

_____

_____

_____

_____

***Washington Crossing the Delaware*, by Emanuel Leutze. On Christmas night, 1776, General George Washington led his troops across the icy Delaware River, a maneuver that surprised the Hessian troops at Trenton and led to a much-needed American victory. This romantic mid-nineteenth-century painting is, however, filled with historical inaccuracies and unlikely poses.** *(Courtesy, The Metropolitan Museum of Art)*

DOCUMENTS ANALYSIS

1. How does the "Cornwallis Country Dance" relate to the Battle of Yorktown in 1781?

_____

_____

_____

_____

_____

_____

CORNWALLIS COUNTRY DANCE. *General Cornwallis's retreat and advance across Carolina and Virginia in 1781 reminded an American balladeer of the contemporary "contre" dance, where two facing lines move back and forth. The English dance tune to which the ballad is set became popular in early nineteenth-century music halls as "Pop Goes the Weasel."*

Cornwallis led a country dance the like was never seen, Sir,
Much retrograde and much advance, and all with General Green, Sir.
They rambled up, they rambled down, joined hands, and off they run, Sir,
   of General Green to Charlestown, the Earl to Wilmington, Sir.

Quoth he, my guards are weary grown with doing country dances.
They never at St. James had shown at capers, kicks, or prances.
No men so gallant there were seen while saunt'ring on parade, Sir,
   or dancing o'er the park so green, or at the masquerades, Sir.

Good Washington, Columbia's sons, whom easy nature taught, Sir,
Now hand in hand they circle round in ev'ry dancing mood, Sir,
The gentle movement soon confounds, the Earl's day draws near, Sir,
   the gentle movement soon confounds, the Earl's day draws near, Sir.

His music soon forgets to play; his feet can't move no more, Sir,
And all his men now curse the day they jigged to our shore, Sir.
Now, Tories all, what can you say . . . Cornwallis is no griper,
But while your hopes are danced away, it's you that pay the piper.

VOCABULARY
The following words may not be part of your normal vocabulary. If their meaning is not familiar to you, you should look them up in a dictionary.

decadence	scrupulous	booty	apportion
pomposity	courtiers	voluble	pall
parody	frivolity	ardor	sedate
untenable	beleaguered	caricature	revelry

IDENTIFICATION OF KEY CONCEPTS
In two to three sentences, identify each of the following:

Battle of Saratoga _____
_____
_____
_____

Battle of Long Island _____
_____
_____
_____

Battle of Trenton _____

_____

_____

French Alliance_____

_____

_____

Battle of Yorktown _____

_____

_____

Treaty of Paris (1783) _____

_____

_____

Articles of Confederation _____

_____

_____

"Critical Period" _____

_____

_____

Jay-Gardoqui Treaty _____

_____

_____

Barbary Pirates _____

_____

_____

Land Ordinance of 1785_____

_____

_____

Northwest Ordinance of 1787 _____

_____

_____

Annapolis Convention _____

_____

_____

manumission of slaves _____
_____
_____
_____

IDENTIFICATION OF KEY INDIVIDUALS

In two to three sentences, identify each of the following:

John Burgoyne _____
_____
_____
_____

John Paul Jones_____
_____
_____
_____

Sally Hemings_____
_____
_____
_____

Benjamin Franklin _____
_____
_____
_____

Benedict Arnold _____
_____
_____
_____

Charles Cornwallis _____
_____
_____
_____

Richard Henry Lee_____
_____
_____
_____

John Dickinson _____
_____
_____
_____

Thomas Jefferson _____

_____

_____

_____

Richard Howe_____

_____

_____

_____

William Howe_____

_____

_____

_____

SELF-TEST
Multiple-Choice Questions

1. In the Peace Treaty of 1783 the British agreed that the western boundary of the United States would be
   a. the Allegheny Mountains.
   b. the Ohio River.
   c. the Rocky Mountains.
   d. the Mississippi River.

2. After the Revolution, Congress prohibited slavery in the
   a. northern states.
   b. Old Northwest.
   c. South.
   d. District of Columbia.

3. Which city was a tight cork bottling up the Mississippi River during the Critical Period?
   a. Vicksburg
   b. St. Louis
   c. Davenport
   d. New Orleans

4. The Northwest Ordinance of 1787
   a. was an idealistic but impractical plan for settling areas north of the Ohio frontier.
   b. had no lasting significance.
   c. established the process by which new states could enter the union.
   d. promised the Iroquois rights to their traditional hunting grounds.

5. The legendary Prussian drillmaster to American troops was
   a. Baron von Steuben.
   b. Thadeuz Kósciuszko.
   c. Herr Schmelling.
   d. Max Baer.

6. Precedent-setting policy for the handling of public lands was contained in the
   a. Land Ordinance of 1785.
   b. Constitution.
   c. Alien and Sedition Acts.
   d. Treaty of Paris.

7. The Dickinson proposals for the Articles of Confederation raised the issue of
   a. giving too much power to the central government.
   b. likely anarchy.
   c. tariffs among the states.
   d. the Louisiana Purchase.

8. Problems in the Critical Period after the Revolution included all but
   a. too much governmental power.
   b. trade problems.
   c. taxation problems.
   d. troubles with Spain and Britain.

9. Undemocratic features that persisted after the Revolution included all but
   a. property ownership as a requirement for voting.
   b. property ownership as a requirement for holding public office.
   c. undemocratic upper houses of state legislatures.
   d. the strengthening of the institution of primogeniture.

10. The early British commanders of their army and navy units in the North were
   a. John Burgoyne and Benedict Arnold.
   b. Nathanael Greene and Baron von Steuben.
   c. Wellington and Marlborough.
   d. the Howe brothers.

Matching Questions
For questions 11 through 15, use one of the lettered items.

11. The American victory that ensured the end of the War for Independence.___
12. The American victory that brought about the Franco-American Alliance.___
13. The American defeat in which Washington avoided complete disaster by quickly and quietly retreating to New Jersey.___
14. The American victory over the Hessians after crossing the Delaware River.___
15. The American defeat outside of Philadelphia in the summer of 1777.___

a. The Battle of Saratoga
b. The Battle of Yorktown
c. The Battle of Brandywine Creek
d. The Battle of Long Island
e. The Battle of Trenton

For questions 16 through 20, use one of the lettered items.

16. The British general who commanded the New York campaigns in 1776 and 1777.___
17. The British general who surrendered at Yorktown.___
18. The American general who eventually betrayed his country.___
19. The French officer who assisted George Washington.___
20. The American naval officer.___

a. Benedict Arnold
b. William Howe
c. Marquis de Lafayette
d. Lord Cornwallis
e. John Paul Jones

True-False Questions
21. The primary British military tactic during the Revolution was a scorched-earth policy that destroyed most American farms and small towns.___
22. George Washington was a general known for hauling through miles of woods his wine cellar, wardrobe, and prostitutes.___
23. Under the Articles of Confederation, the states could do nothing about the Barbary Pirates.___

24. Because of the Revolution, several states either abolished or placed restrictions on the ownership of slaves.____
25. In 1787 most Americans worked relatively self-sufficient farms.____

Essay Questions

1. "The American Revolution was a conservative movement." Explain your reasons for agreeing or disagreeing with this view.

_____
_____
_____
_____
_____
_____
_____
_____
_____
_____
_____
_____
_____

2. Name some weaknesses of the United States under the Articles of Confederation.

_____
_____
_____
_____
_____
_____
_____
_____
_____
_____
_____
_____
_____

Self-Test Answers

1. d 2. b 3. d 4. c 5. a 6. a 7. a 8. a 9. d 10. d 11. b 12. a
13. d 14. e 15. c 16. b 17. d 18. a 19. c 20. e 21. F 22. F
23. T 24. T 25. T

WE THE PEOPLE 1787–1800

SUGGESTED OUTCOMES

After studying Chapter 6, you should be able to

1. Explain the major debates and compromises at the Constitutional Convention.
2. Describe the process by which the Constitution was ratified as well as the philosophical arguments of the Federalists and Anti-Federalists.
3. Explain the background of the Bill of Rights.
4. Describe Alexander Hamilton's economic views, how he planned to use the federal government to implement them, and how successful he was in achieving his goals.
5. Explain the reasons behind the Whiskey Rebellion.
6. Compare and contrast the Hamiltonian and Jeffersonian philosophies.
7. Explain how the French Revolution became an influence in American politics.
8. Describe the early development of political parties in the United States.
9. Describe the foreign policy problems the United States had with France and Great Britain in the 1790s.
10. Evaluate the successes and failures of the Adams Administration.
11. Describe the election of 1800 and its significance.
12. Explain the significance of Shays's Rebellion.

CHRONOLOGY

1786 Shays's Rebellion erupts in western Massachusetts.
The Annapolis Convention meets.

1787 The Constitutional Convention meets in Philadelphia.

1788 James Madison, Alexander Hamilton, and John Jay write *The Federalist Papers*.

1789 Eleven states—with the exceptions of Rhode Island and North Carolina—ratify the new Constitution.
George Washington becomes first President of the United States.
The first Congress of the United States meets.
The French Revolution erupts.

1790 Alexander Hamilton issues his *Report Relative to Public Credit*, proposing funding the national debt and the federal assumption of the state debts.

1791 Alexander Hamilton issues his *Report on a National Bank*.
Alexander Hamilton issues his *Report on Manufactures*.
The Bank of the United States is established.
The first ten amendments, or Bill of Rights, are added to the Constitution.

1793 Britain begins to seize American ships engaged in trade with France.
The Citizen Genet affair creates a political firestorm in the United States.

1794 The Whiskey Rebellion occurs in Pennsylvania.

1795 Jay's Treaty is negotiated with Great Britain.
Pinckney's Treaty is negotiated with Spain.

1796 Washington gives his Farewell Address.
John Adams is elected second President of the United States.

1798 Publication of the XYZ Affair creates animosity in America toward France. Congress passes the Alien and Sedition Acts.

James Madison writes the Virginia Resolution and Thomas Jefferson writes the Kentucky Resolution.

1800 Washington, D.C., becomes the capital of the United States.

PHOTOGRAPH AND ILLUSTRATION ANALYSIS

1. Look at the accompanying illustration. Explain the historical background of the event the illustration is portraying.

_____

_____

_____

_____

_____

_____

_____

_____

The tarring and feathering of an excise officer during the Whiskey Rebellion (*Courtesy, Brown Brothers*)

2. Look at the following illustration. Explain the historical background of the event the illustration is portraying.

_____

_____

_____

_____

_____

_____
_____
_____
_____

In the summer of 1786, farmers' discontent over taxes broke into rebellion when Daniel Shays and his band attacked state troops at Springfield, Massachusetts, an action that was soon quelled. *(Drawing by Howard Pyle, Courtesy, The Libraru of Congress)*

DOCUMENTS ANALYSIS

1. Read Abigail Adams's description of Washington, D.C., when she first arrived there in 1800. What were her impressions of the city?

_____

_____

_____

_____

_____

_____

Washington, 21 November, 1800.

. . . I arrived here on Sunday last, and without meeting with any accident worth noticing, except losing ourselves when we left Baltimore, and going eight or nine miles on the Frederick road, by which means we were obliged to go the other eight through woods, where we wandered two hours without finding a guide, or the path. Fortunately, a straggling black came up with us, and we engaged him as a guide, to extricate us out of our difficulty; but woods are all you see, from Baltimore until you reach [Washington]. . . .

The President's house is upon a grand and superb scale, requiring about thirty servants to attend and keep the apartments in proper order, and perform the ordinary business of the house and stables; an establishment very well proportioned to the President's salary. The lighting the apartments, from the kitchen to parlours and chambers, is a tax indeed; and the fires we are obliged to keep to secure us from daily agues is another very cheering comfort. . . . If they will put me up some bells, and let me have wood enough to keep fires, I design to be pleased. I could content myself almost anywhere three months; but, surrounded with forests, can you believe that wood is not to be had, because people cannot be found to cut and cart it! Briesler entered into a contract with a man to supply him with wood. A small part, a few cords only, has he been able to get. Most of that was expended to dry the walls of the house before we came in, and yesterday the man told him it was impossible for him to procure it to be cut and carted. He has had recourse to coals; but we cannot get grates made and set. We have, indeed, come into _a new country_.

VOCABULARY

The following words may not be part of your normal vocabulary. If their meaning is not familiar to you, you should look them up in a dictionary.

gauntlet	ratify	excise	aghast
monarchical	exuberant	privateer	frigate
arsenal	thoroughfare	partisan	anarchy
musket	licentiousness	sovereignty	unscrupulous
federalism	gullible	emissary	rogue
impasse	polity	arbitration	
tyrannical	congruent	libel	

IDENTIFICATION OF KEY CONCEPTS

In two to three sentences, identify each of the following:

Shays's Rebellion _____

_____

_____

_____

Virginia Plan _____

_____

_____

New Jersey Plan _____
_____
_____
_____

Connecticut Plan _____
_____
_____
_____

federalism _____
_____
_____
_____

checks and balances _____
_____
_____
_____

The Federalist Papers _____
_____
_____
_____

Bill of Rights _____
_____
_____
_____

Whiskey Rebellion _____
_____
_____
_____

French Revolution _____
_____
_____
_____

Jay's Treaty _____
_____
_____
_____

Election of 1800 _____
_____
_____
_____

XYZ Affair _____

_____

_____

Alien and Sedition Acts _____

_____

_____

Virginia and Kentucky Resolutions _____

_____

_____

Hamiltonian political philosophy _____

_____

_____

Jeffersonian political philosophy _____

_____

_____

Washington's Farewell Address _____

_____

_____

_____

IDENTIFICATION OF KEY INDIVIDUALS

In two to three sentences, identify each of the following:

Daniel Shays _____

_____

_____

James Madison _____

_____

_____

John Jay _____

_____

_____

Alexander Hamilton _____
_____
_____
_____

Timothy Pickering _____
_____
_____
_____

Citizen Genet _____
_____
_____
_____

John Adams_____
_____
_____
_____

SELF-TEST

Multiple-Choice Questions

1. The Constitution of 1787 gave Congress all these powers except
   a. review over the consitutionality of immigration laws.
   b. taxation.
   c. the right to coin money.
   d. regulation of interstate commerce.

2. The newspaper articles later known as *The Federalist Papers* were written by
   a. Jefferson, Madison, and Adams.
   b. Madison, Adams, and Washington.
   c. Madison, Jefferson, and Jay.
   d. Madison, Hamilton, and Jay.

3. Debate over ratification of the Constitution centered around
   a. Hamilton's plan for the United States.
   b. the government's right to tax.
   c. federal power and personal freedom.
   d. the Virginia and Connecticut Plans.

4. Major Pierre L'Enfant
   a. demanded tribute from the United States for France.
   b. fought a duel with Aaron Burr.
   c. experimented with inoculation against smallpox.
   d. designed Washington, D.C.

5. Hamilton's economic plan included all of the following except
   a. a national bank.
   b. assumption of state debts.
   c. funding the national debt.
   d. agricultural subsidies.

6. During the 1780s most nationalists sought
   a. to increase the authority of state legislatures.
   b. to admit the western territories to statehood as quickly as possible.
   c. no change in the Articles of Confederation.
   d. to strengthen the central government.

7. Britain's war with France in the 1790s initially
   a. had little effect on American shipping.
   b. endangered the American economy by limiting trade.
   c. promoted American shipping because the United States was a neutral carrier.
   d. virtually destroyed all American shipping.

8. The Virginia and Kentucky Resolutions
   a. renewed the debate on the tensions between federal authority and the rights of the states.
   b. forced the Federalists to create the Alien and Sedition Acts.
   c. called for the reorganization of the national government.
   d. accepted the Alien Act as a matter of national defense, but condemned the Sedition Act as a violation of personal freedom.

9. Shays's Rebellion occurred in
   a. Maine.
   b. western Massachusetts.
   c. Pennsylvania.
   d. Georgia.

10. The Founding Father whose wishes come closest to today's reality of a strong central government is
    a. Thomas Jefferson.
    b. Alexander Hamilton.
    c. George Pinckney.
    d. James Monroe.

Matching Questions

For questions 11 through 15, use one of the lettered items.

11. Attempted to limit attacks on individual rights by proclaiming states' rights.___
12. Cleared the northwestern forts of British troops.___
13. Gave the United States use of New Orleans as a port.___
14. Nearly precipitated war with France.___
15. A Federalist attempt to crush all political opposition in the late 1790s.___

a. Alien and Sedition Acts
b. XYZ Affair
c. Virginia and Kentucky Resolutions
d. Jay's Treaty
e. Pinckney's Treaty

For questions 16 through 20, use one of the lettered items.

16. The second president of the United States.___
17. Author of *The Federalist Papers* and the man who negotiated a treaty with Great Britain in 1795.___
18. The man of questionable moral values who tied Thomas Jefferson for President in the election of 1800 but lost the election in the House of Representatives.___
19. The French diplomat whose activities enraged the Washington administration.___
20. Author of *The Federalist Papers* and secretary of the treasury under George Washington.___

a. John Adams
b. Alexander Hamilton
c. Citizen Genet
d. John Jay
e. Aaron Burr

True-False Questions

21. Political parties first acquired considerable strength under the administration of John Adams.___
22. In the election of 1796, no candidate received a plurality of electoral votes for president.___
23. The Bill of Rights reserves to the national government powers not specifically awarded to the states.___
24. Shays's Rebellion was a revolt of debt-pressed farmers.___
25. The Jeffersonians favored state over national power, agriculture over industry, and a "strict" over "loose" construction of the Constitution.___

Essay Questions

1. Some have suggested that if the United States had convened a Constitutional Convention today as it did in 1787, the fundamental problems of how properly to balance order and liberty would dominate as they had in 1787. What concerns would have been in evidence today? Compare the debate over "liberty and order" in the convention in 1787 with what it might be today.

_____
_____
_____
_____
_____
_____
_____
_____
_____
_____
_____
_____
_____
_____
_____
_____
_____
_____
_____
_____
_____
_____
_____
_____
_____
_____
_____

2. As a revolutionary leader forced to choose between the programs favored by Jefferson and those favored by Hamilton, which would you have chosen? Why? Which program, Hamilton's or Jefferson's, best expressed the needs of American society?

_____

_____

_____

_____

_____

_____

_____

_____

_____

_____

_____

_____

_____

_____

_____

_____

_____

_____

_____

_____

_____

_____

_____

_____

_____

_____

_____

_____

_____

Self-Test Answers

1. a 2. d 3. c 4. d 5. d 6. d 7. b 8. a 9. b 10. b 11. c 12. d
13. e 14. b 15. a 16. a 17. d 18. e 19. c 20. b 21. T 22. F
23. F 24. T 25. T

 # INDEPENDENCE CONFIRMED
1800–1816

SUGGESTED OUTCOMES

After studying Chapter 7, you should be able to
1. Explain the significance of the Lewis and Clark expedition.
2. Describe life in American cities in the early 1800s.
3. Describe farm life in America in the early 1800s.
4. Explain Thomas Jefferson's belief in limited government.
5. Explain why France sold the Louisiana Territory to the United States and its significance in American history.
6. Describe the causes of the War of 1812.
7. Explain why the War Hawks wanted war.
8. Explain why historians believe there was no victor in the War of 1812.
9. Explain how the American victory at New Orleans took place *after* the end of the war.

CHRONOLOGY

1800 Thomas Jefferson is elected third President of the United States.

1801 John Marshall becomes chief justice of the Supreme Court.

1803 The Supreme Court decides the *Marbury v. Madison* case.
Thomas Jefferson completes the Louisiana Purchase.

1804 The Lewis and Clark expedition begins.
Aaron Burr kills Alexander Hamilton in a duel.

1806 Lewis and Clark expedition ends.
The Zebulon Pike expedition begins.
Napoleon issues the Berlin Decree.

1807 Congress passes the Embargo Act.
The British navy begins impressing American sailors.

1808 Congress outlaws the African slave trade.
James Madison is elected President of the United States.

1809 Congress repeals the Embargo Act of 1807.
Congress passes the Non-Intercourse Act.

1810 Congress passes Macon's Bill No. 2.
The "War Hawks" enter Congress.

1811 Battle of Tippecanoe occurs.
President James Madison refuses to renew the charter of the Bank of the United States.

1812 Congress declares war on Great Britain.
James Madison is reelected to a second term.

1813 Battle of Lake Erie occurs.
Battle of the Thames occurs.

1814 Battle of Horseshoe Bend takes place.
British troops burn Washington, D.C.
Battle of Lake Champlain occurs.
The Treaty of Ghent is signed ending the War of 1812.

1815 The Battle of New Orleans occurs.

1816 Congress establishes the Second Bank of the United States.
James Monroe is elected fifth President of the United States.

PHOTOGRAPH AND ILLUSTRATION ANALYSIS

1. Look at these sketches of Indians. What do they reveal about American attitudes toward Indians in the early 1800s?

_____

_____

_____

_____

_____

_____

Lewis and Clark holding a council with the Indians. Their expedition was prompted by President Jefferson's vision of an America stretching from "the Western ocean . . . to the Atlantic." This drawing is from the 1812 edition of Patrick Gass's *Journal*, one of the first authentic accounts of the expedition. *(Courtesy, Scribner's Archives)*

Tecumseh saving white prisoners. Despite his martial intentions, he was known for his revulsion at senseless cruelty. *(Courtesy, Henry E. Huntington Library and Art Gallery)*

DOCUMENTS ANALYSIS

1. Read Meriwether Lewis's description of Shoshone family life. What was life like for men compared to women?

_____
_____
_____
_____
_____
_____

They seldom correct their children particularly the boys who soon become masters of their own acts. They give as a reason that it cows and breaks the sperit of the boy to whip him, and that he never recovers his independence of mind after he is grown. They treat their women but with little rispect, and compel them to perform every species of drudgery. they collect the wild fruits and roots, attend to the horses or assist in that duty, cook, dress the skins and make all their apparel, collect wood and make their fires, arrange and form their lodges, and when they travel pack the horses and take charge of all the baggage; in short the man dose little else except attend his horses hunt and fish. the man considers himself degraded if he is compelled to walk any distance; and if he is so unfortunately poor as only to possess two horses he rides the best himself and leavs the woman or women if he has more than one, to transport their baggage and children on the other, and to walk if the horse is unable to carry the additional weight of their persons. The chastity of their women is not held in high estimation, and the husband will for a trifle barter the companion of his bed for a night or longer if he conceives the reward adequate.

2. Read the letters. What do they reveal about American attitudes toward women in the early 1800s?

_____

_____

_____

_____

_____

_____

A WOMAN'S PLACE IN JEFFERSONIAN AMERICA: INFANTS IN CHURCH. *This vignette, composed of letters to the editor of the* Independent Mechanic *(1811), ultimately reveals great male condescension towards women. But perhaps in Ms. Sarah Touchstone, who is not blameless, the "Friend to Females" has met his match.*

Mr. Editor,

I know of no subject which deserves more to be noticed, than that of women taking their infants to church. No woman will expose her bare bosom to a gaping multitude of men; and this she is necessitated to do frequently, in order to pacify her babe. Indeed, often it is the case, that when the minister in the sacred desk, is in the most solemn, affecting, and interesting part of his discourse; and when too his audience are loath to hear the sound of a footstep, fearful that they may lose the train of his reasoning, and when the whole congregation are in the most respectful silence, that the ears of all are stunned, the imaginations confused, and the soul tortured by cries and screeches of an infant. What, I ask, is more vexatious? What can be more painful? . . . Besides, other evil consequences flow from it: many an infant receives a death-cold, from their being wrapped up warm in church, and after service are exposed to the damp dews of night and chilling blasts. That mother who possesses a tender feeling for her babe will not sport with its health. May this short notice be received as friendly advice from one who is a

FRIEND TO FEMALES

Independent Mechanic, December 21, 1811

Mr. Editor:

I would beg leave through the medium of your paper, to address a few lines to answer to a morose old jockey who came out in your last in the character of "A FRIEND TO FEMALES."

I cannot say that I thank the gentleman for his pretended friendly advice; and as no person can like their church better than I do, I must attend as often as my family affairs will permit. After having paid this tribute of my God, I feel as happy through the week as possible. I feel as if I had something very heavy taken from my breast. I am sure that my son (God bless his little dimpled cheeks!) never disturbed any one of the congregation, although he is my companion at the house of God. Even while I am writing, it is smiling in my face as if it knew its injured mother busied in vindicating her wrongs. . . .

"Expose her bosom to a gaping multitude of men." A gaping multitude of men, did he say? Yes; and I am sorry to be under the disagreeable necessity of joining with him in the assertion; for how many deluded wretches are there, who only enter the house of the Lord to gape, and put female modesty to the blush, by their rude behaviour. If they came there to hear the word of God, they would not be gaping at the mother's naked bosom. He says— "when the minister is in the most interesting part of his discourse, the ears of the congregation are stunned by the cries and screeches of an infant" a most wonderful *infant,* that can stun the ears of a whole congregation with its weak and unfinished organs, and prevent him from hearing the preacher! Upon my word, I never heard such absurdity in my life.

SARAH TOUCHSTONE

Independent Mechanic, December 28, 1811

3. Read the comments. Did politics affect the way leaders felt about one another? Why could someone say that politics today may actually not be as nasty as it was 200 years ago?

_____

_____

_____

_____

_____

_____

_____

_____

_____

_____

_____

_____

BROTHERLY LOVE AMONG THE FOUNDING FATHERS

John Adams on Thomas Jefferson: "[He has] a mind, soured, yet seeking for popularity, and eaten to a honeycomb with ambition, yet weak, confused, uninformed, and ignorant."

—on Alexander Hamilton: "This man is stark mad, or I am." "[Consider] the profligacy of his life; his fornications, adulteries and his incests."

—on Benjamin Franklin: "His whole life has been one continued insult to good manners and to decency. . . . From five complete years of experience of Dr. Franklin . . . I can have no dependence on his word. . . . I wish with all my soul he was out of public service."

Thomas Jefferson on Adams: "[He is] distrustful, obstinate, excessively vain, and takes no counsel from anyone."

—on Hamilton: "I will not suffer my retirement to be clouded by the slanders of a man whose history, from the moment at which history can stoop to notice him, is a tissue of machinations against the liberty of the country which not only has received and given him bread, but heaped its honors on his head."

Alexander Hamilton on Jefferson: "A man of profound ambition and violent passions . . . the most intriguing man in the United States . . . the intriguing incendiary, the aspiring turbulent competitor . . . prone to projects which are incompatible with the principles of stable and systematic government."

—on Adams: ". . . disgusting egotism . . . distempered jealousy . . . ungovernable indiscretion." ". . . vanity without bounds."

MAP ANALYSIS

1. Look at the map below, which indicates the paths of the Lewis and Clark expedition and the Zebulon Pike expedition. What contemporary states did the expeditions cross? Why did both groups seem to stay so close to major rivers during their journeys?

_____

_____

_____

_____

_____

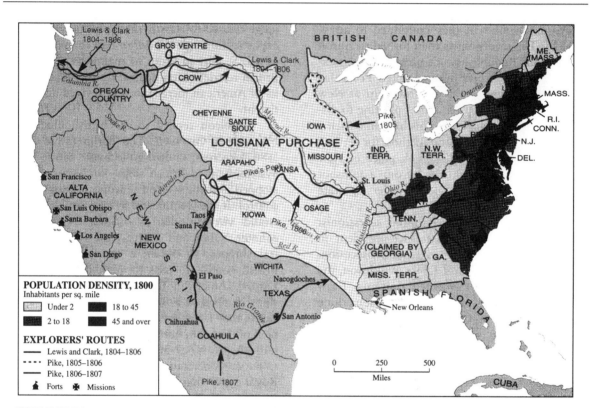

THE LOUISIANA PURCHASE. In 1802, Jefferson predicted that the lands of the great Mississippi Valley "from its fertility . . . will ere long yield half of our whole produce, and contain more than half of our whole population." "The day that France takes possession of New Orleans," the President warned, "we must marry ourselves to the British fleet and nation." To prevent this outcome, he purchased Louisiana from Napoleon I for $15 million.

VOCABULARY

The following words may not be part of your normal vocabulary. If their meaning is not familiar to you, you should look them up in a dictionary.

lexicon	recalcitrant	temporize	calamity
ichthyologist	pacifist	cache	plummet
ornithologist	disavow	logistical	grapeshot
entrepreneur	reparation	skirmish	leverage
almanacs	belligerent	flotilla	stigma
consummation	wizened	impunity	

IDENTIFICATION OF KEY CONCEPTS

In two to three sentences, identify each of the following:

Lewis and Clark Expedition_____
_____
_____
_____

Northwest Passage _____
_____
_____

Thomas Jefferson and Monticello _____
_____
_____
_____

*Marbury v. Madison*_____
_____
_____
_____

Louisiana Purchase_____
_____
_____
_____

Republican adoption of Federalist views _____
_____
_____
_____

judicial review_____
_____
_____
_____

impressment _____
_____
_____
_____

Embargo Act of 1807 _____
_____
_____
_____

Non-Intercourse Act of 1809 _____

_____

_____

_____

Macon's Bill No. 2 _____

_____

_____

War Hawks _____

_____

_____

Treaty of Ghent _____

_____

_____

Battle of New Orleans _____

_____

_____

_____

IDENTIFICATION OF KEY INDIVIDUALS

In two to three sentences, identify each of the following:

Meriwether Lewis_____

_____

_____

_____

Zebulon Pike_____

_____

_____

_____

John Marshall _____

_____

_____

_____

Toussaint L'Ouverture _____

_____

_____

_____

James Monroe_____

_____

_____

_____

Aaron Burr _____
_____
_____
_____

Tecumseh _____
_____
_____
_____

Oliver Perry _____
_____
_____
_____

SELF-TEST

Multiple-Choice Questions

1. The largest city in the United States in 1800 was
   a. Boston.
   b. Charleston.
   c. Washington.
   d. Philadelphia.

2. Thomas Jefferson's classic revival home is called
   a. the Hermitage.
   b. Hyde Park.
   c. Sagamore Hill.
   d. Monticello.

3. The United States purchased Louisiana from
   a. Spain.
   b. Great Britain.
   c. Portugal.
   d. France.

4. Some of the War Hawks wanted the United States to annex
   a. Mexico.
   b. Canada.
   c. Nicaragua.
   d. Alaska.

5. Many New Englanders opposed the War of 1812 because
   a. it threatened to interfere with commerce.
   b. they depended on trade with native Americans.
   c. they were pacifists.
   d. they had not had time to rebuild ships destroyed in the American Revolution.

6. Which of the following statements about the Jefferson Administration is false?
   a. It reduced the size of the army.
   b. It reduced federal spending.
   c. It planned for a more active national economy.
   d. It allowed the Sedition Act to lapse.

7. The Treaty of Ghent ending the War of 1812
   a. was a victory for the British.
   b. was a victory for the United States.
   c. restored the situation as it had existed before the war.
   d. was never formally signed.

8. Chief Justice Marshall
   a. supported the federal government over those of the states.
   b. supported the power of the states over that of the federal government.
   c. hindered cheap transportation by supporting steamboat monopolies.
   d. did little of lasting importance.

9. American conduct in the War of 1812 can best be characterized as
   a. ill-planned and badly managed.
   b. successful on land but not on sea.
   c. a demonstration that European military tactics did not work in the New World.
   d. a case of dangerous indifference.

10. The War of 1812 resulted in part from all of these issues except
    a. impressment of American seamen.
    b. conflict over neutral rights.
    c. a British proclamation of a new series of Orders in Council in June 1812.
    d. British provocation of Indian attacks.

Matching Questions

For questions 11 through 15, use one of the lettered items.

11. A major American victory *after* the War of 1812 was already over.___
12. A British victory that resulted in the burning of Buffalo.___
13. The American defeat of the Indians under Tecumseh.___
14. The American defeat caused primarily by hesitancy.___
15. The American naval victory under Oliver Perry.___

   a. Battle of New Orleans
   b. Battle of Lake Erie
   c. Battle of Tippecanoe Creek
   d. Battle of Fort George
   e. Battle of the Niagara Frontier

For questions 16 through 20, use one of the lettered items.

16. Firmly established the principle of judicial review.___
17. Prohibited American ships from sailing to foreign ports.___
18. Permitted American ships to sail anywhere in the world except ports in England and France.___
19. A French order requiring the seizure of any ships carrying British goods.___
20. Allowed the President to reopen trade with England and France and, if one of them agreed to modify its trade policies, to reimpose the embargo on the other.___

   a. Berlin Decree
   b. Macon's Bill No. 2
   c. Embargo Act of 1807
   d. Non-Intercourse Act of 1809
   e. *Marbury v. Madison*

True-False Questions

21. The Embargo Act of 1807, like the embargoes during the Revolutionary era, had a disastrous impact on the British economy.___
22. Thomas Jefferson believed in a strong central government and weak states' rights.___
23. Alexander Hamilton and John Marshall wanted to build a strong central government for the United States.___
24. Had it not been for Andrew Jackson's victory at the Battle of New Orleans, the United States would have lost the War of 1812.___
25. The British burning of Washington, D.C., in the War of 1812 was in retaliation for the American burning of York, Canada.___

Essay Questions

1. Evidence of a likely sexual liaison between Thomas Jefferson and Sally Hemings raises exactly those fears white southerners had about the intermingling of the races. Now that the United States is a multicultural society with frequent intermarriages across religions, cultures, and races, the fears of the white South have largely receded into the distant past. Does Jefferson's "transgression" with Sally Hemings legitimize the nation's future? What elements in Jefferson's thinking are justified by his affair with Sally? With the nation of Jefferson now so diverse, what can be done to unify it?

_____

_____

_____

_____

_____

_____

_____

_____

_____

_____

_____

_____

_____

_____

_____

_____

_____

_____

_____

_____

_____

_____

_____

_____

_____

_____

_____

_____

_____

_____

_____

_____

_____

_____

_____

_____

_____

2. Jefferson envisioned a nation of independent farmers who drew their strength and character from nature and the soil. Ours is a society in which most Americans work for someone else and live in cities, but the attractions to rural life remain quite strong. From cowboy movies to the modern ecology movement, our culture is filled with signs that Americans still believe that Jefferson's world of simplicity and nature is the more valued America. Examine the signs in our society and culture of the continuing lure of the Jeffersonian appeal. Is there not a danger that in our increasingly technological and urbanized world this attachment to nature will cause unnecessary personal and social problems? Should it be abandoned?

_____
_____
_____
_____
_____
_____
_____
_____
_____
_____
_____
_____
_____
_____
_____
_____
_____
_____
_____
_____
_____
_____
_____
_____

Self-Test Answers

1. d 2. d 3. d 4. b 5. a 6. c 7. c 8. a 9. a 10. c 11. a 12. e
13. c 14. d 15. b 16. e 17. c 18. d 19. a 20. b 21. F 22. F
23. T 24. F 25. T

SINEWS OF NATIONHOOD

SUGGESTED OUTCOMES

After studying Chapter 8, you should be able to

1. Describe the economic impact of the construction of the Erie Canal on the northeastern region of the United States.
2. Describe the "Transportation Revolution" and the role of turnpikes, canals, steamboats, and railroads in American life.
3. Describe the rise of the factory system in early America.
4. Describe the major inventions that changed American farming in the first half of the nineteenth century.
5. Explain the reasons for the decline of the Federalist Party in the early 1800s.
6. Explain what is meant by the term "Era of Good Feelings."
7. Describe how and why the role of the federal government in economic affairs increased after the War of 1812.
8. Explain the causes of the Panic of 1819 and why the Second Bank of the United States was blamed.
9. Describe the decisions of the Supreme Court that established the power of the federal government and the sanctity of contracts in the early 1800s.

CHRONOLOGY

1807	Robert Fulton invents the steamboat.
1810	*Fletcher v. Peck*
1811	Charter of the first Bank of the United States expires.
1814–15	Hartford Convention takes place.
1816	James Monroe is elected President.
	Congress passes the Tariff of 1816.
	The Second Bank of the United States is chartered.
1819	The Panic of 1819 occurs.
	Dartmouth College v. Woodward
	McCulloch v. Maryland
1820	James Monroe is reelected to a second term.
1821	*Cohens v. Virginia*
1823	Nicholas Biddle becomes president of the Second Bank of the United States.
1824	*Gibbons v. Ogden*

DOCUMENTS AND PHOTOGRAPH ANALYSIS

1. Read this selection by James Fenimore Cooper. Why is it an early example of environmental concern in America?

_____

_____

_____

_____

_____

_____

SHOOTING PIGEONS *by James Fenimore Cooper*

Amidst the hurly-burly of national politics, the environmental splendors of the United States were already under attack. James Fenimore Cooper (1789–1851), born in upstate New York, wrote the Leather-stocking Tales, *a series of five novels about life on the American frontier. The series takes its name from its hero, a woodsman who is variously called Natty Bumppo, Deerslayer, Hawkeye, Pathfinder, Leather-stocking, and the "trapper."*

This excerpt, taken from Pioneers *(1823), describes a pigeon hunt. The passage furnishes one of the earliest lessons in environmentalism to be found in American literature. Cooper perceived the limits of the seemingly inexhaustible American landscape.*

If the heavens were alive with pigeons, the whole village seemed equally in motion with men, women, and children. Every species of fire-arms, from the French ducking-gun with a barrel near six feet in length, to the common horseman's pistol, was to be seen in the hands of the men and boys; while bows and arrows, some made of the simple stick of a walnut sapling, and others in a rude imitation of the ancient cross-bows, were carried by many of the latter.

The houses and the signs of life apparent in the village, drove the alarmed birds from the direct line of their flight, toward the mountains, along the sides and near the bases of which they were glancing in dense masses, equally wonderful by the rapidity of their motion, and their incredible numbers. . . .

Across the inclined plane which fell from the steep ascent of the mountain to the banks of the Susquehanna, ran the highway, on either side of which a clearing of many acres had been made at a very early day. Over those clearings, and up the eastern mountain, and along the dangerous path that was cut into its side, the different individuals posted themselves, and in a few moments that attack commenced.

Among the sportsmen was the tall, gaunt form of Leather-stocking, walking over the field, with his rifle hanging on his arm, his dogs at his heels; the latter now scenting the dead or wounded birds, that were beginning to tumble from the flocks, and then crouching under the legs of their master, as if they participated in his feelings at this wasteful and unsportsmanlike execution.

The reports of the fire-arms became rapid, whole volleys rising from the plain, as flocks of more than ordinary numbers darted over the opening, shadowing the field like a cloud; and then the light smoke of a single piece would issue from among the leafless bushes on the mountain, as death was hurled on the retreat of the affrighted birds, who were rising from a volley, in a vain effort to escape. Arrows, and missiles of every kind, were in the midst of the flocks; and so numerous were the birds, and so low did they take their flight, that even long poles, in the hands of those on the sides of the mountain, were used to strike them to the earth. . . .

Among the relics of the old military excursions, that occasionally are discovered throughout the different districts of the western part of New-York, there had been found . . . a small swivel, which would carry a ball of a pound weight. . . . This miniature cannon had been released from the rust, and being mounted on little wheels, was now in a state for actual service. For several years it was the sole organ for extraordinary rejoicings used in those mountains. On the mornings of the Fourths of July, it would be heard ringing among the hills. . . .

"An't the woods his work as well as the pigeons? Use, but don't waste. Wasn't the woods made for the beasts and birds to harbor in? And when man wanted their flesh, their skins, or their feathers, there's the place to seek them. But I'll go to the hut with my own game, for I wouldn't touch one of the harmless things that cover the ground here, looking up with their eyes on me, as if they only wanted tongues to say their thoughts."

With this sentiment in his mouth, Leather-stocking threw his rifle over his arm, and followed by his dogs, stepped across the clearing with great caution, taking care not to tread on one of the wounded birds in his path. He soon entered the bushes on the margin of the lake, and was hid from view.

---

2. Look at the "Time Table of the Lowell Mills." From that document, what can you tell about the living arrangements of the Lowell workers? Also, look at the photograph of Lowell workers on the next page. What does it tell you about their daily work?

_____

_____

_____

_____

_____

_____

_____

_____

_____

TIME TABLE OF THE LOWELL MILLS,

Arranged to make the working time throughout the year average 11 hours per day.

TO TAKE EFFECT SEPTEMBER 21st., 1853.

The Standard time being that of the meridian of Lowell, as shown by the Regulator Clock of AMOS SANBORN, Post Office Corner, Central Street.

From March 20th to September 19th, inclusive.

COMMENCE WORK, at 6.30 A. M. LEAVE OFF WORK, at 6.30 P. M., except on Saturday Evenings.
BREAKFAST at 6 A. M. DINNER, at 12 M. Commence Work, after dinner, 12.45 P. M.

From September 20th to March 19th, inclusive.

COMMENCE WORK at 7.00 A. M. LEAVE OFF WORK, at 7.00 P. M., except on Saturday Evenings.
BREAKFAST at 6.30 A. M. DINNER, at 12.30 P.M. Commence Work, after dinner, 1.15 P. M.

BELLS.

From March 20th to September 19th, inclusive.

Morning Bells.	Dinner Bells.	Evening Bells.
First bell,..........4.30 A. M.	Ring out,..............12.00 M.	Ring out,..........6.30 P. M.
Second, 5.30 A. M. ; Third, 6.20.	Ring in,..........12 35 P. M.	Except on Saturday Evenings.

From September 20th to March 19th, inclusive.

Morning Bells.	Dinner Bells.	Evening Bells.
First bell,..........5.00 A. M.	Ring out,..........12.30 P. M.	Ring out at..........7.00 P. M.
Second, 6.00 A. M. ; Third, 6.50.	Ring in,..............1.05 P. M.	Except on Saturday Evenings.

SATURDAY EVENING BELLS.

During APRIL, MAY, JUNE, JULY, and AUGUST, Ring Out, at 6.00 P. M.
The remaining Saturday Evenings in the year, ring out as follows :

SEPTEMBER.	NOVEMBER.	JANUARY.
First Saturday, ring out 6.00 P. M.	Third Saturday ring out 4.00 P. M.	Third Saturday, ring out 4.25 P. M.
Second " " 5.45 "	Fourth " " 3.55 "	Fourth " " 4.35 "
Third " " 5.30 "		
Fourth " " 5.20 "	DECEMBER.	FEBRUARY.
	First Saturday, ring out 3.50 P. M.	First Saturday, ring out 4.45 P. M.
OCTOBER.	Second " " 3.55 "	Second " " 4.55 "
First Saturday, ring out 5.05 P. M.	Third " " 3.55 "	Third " " 5.00 "
Second " " 4.55 "	Fourth " " 4.00 "	Fourth " " 5.10 "
Third " " 4.45 "	Fifth " " 4.00 "	
Fourth " " 4.35 "		MARCH.
Fifth " " 4.25 "	JANUARY.	First Saturday, ring out 5.25 P. M.
NOVEMBER.	First Saturday, ring out 4.10 P. M.	Second " " 5.30 "
First Saturday, ring out 4.15 P. M.	Second " " 4.15 "	Third " " 5.35 "
Second "· " 4.05 "		Fourth " " 5.45 "

YARD GATES will be opened at the first stroke of the bells for entering or leaving the Mills.

•.• *SPEED GATES commence hoisting three minutes before commencing work.*

Penhallow, Printer, Wyman's Exchange, 28 Merrimack St.

New England farm daughters, and later Irish immigrants, comprised much of the nation's first factory workforce. The young mill women who worked in this New England textile mill stopped work to pose for this early view, ca. 1850. *(Courtesy, International Museum of Photography, George Eastman House)*

3. Look at the photograph of the slave family. What does it tell you about their living arrangements? Do you think they were worse off or better off than the Lowell factory workers?

_____

_____

_____

_____

_____

A slave family in the cotton fields of Georgia. *(Courtesy, New-York Historical Society)*

IDENTIFICATION OF KEY CONCEPTS

In two to three sentences, identify each of the following:

Transportation Revolution _____
_____
_____
_____

interchangeable parts _____
_____
_____
_____

Erie Canal _____
_____
_____
_____

Waltham System _____
_____
_____
_____

Era of Good Feelings _____
_____
_____
_____

internal improvements _____
_____
_____
_____

Panic of 1819 _____
_____
_____

Gibbons v. Ogden _____
_____
_____

Dartmouth College v. Woodward _____
_____
_____
_____

Hartford Convention _____

_____

_____

_____

Tariff of 1816 _____

_____

_____

_____

IDENTIFICATION OF KEY INDIVIDUALS

In two to three sentences, identify each of the following:

Alexis de Tocqueville _____

_____

_____

_____

Robert Fulton _____

_____

_____

_____

Francis Cabot Lowell _____

_____

_____

_____

Cyrus McCormick _____

_____

_____

_____

John Deere _____

_____

_____

_____

Eli Whitney_____

_____

_____

_____

Nicholas Biddle_____

_____

_____

_____

John Marshall _____

_____

_____

_____

NAME _____ DATE _____

Albert Gallatin _____
_____
_____
_____

VOCABULARY

The following words may not be part of your normal vocabulary. If their meaning is not familiar to you, you should look them up in a dictionary.

terminus	primeval	benevolence	nationalist
itinerary	ingenuity	audacious	depreciate
microcosm	paternalistic	aggrandizement	
forage	genteel	orthodoxy	

SELF-TEST

Multiple-Choice Questions

1. During the Era of Good Feelings
   a. there was only one major political party, but factional rivalries persisted.
   b. there were two major parties, but they agreed on most issues.
   c. the United States had its only experiment with a three-party system.
   d. American expansionism was temporarily halted.

2. The Panic of 1819 occurred because of
   a. the restrictive policies of the Bank of the United States.
   b. continuing trade restrictions with European countries.
   c. a postwar spirit of extravagance and speculation.
   d. the tariff of 1816.

3. The development of steamboats, which made it economically feasible to bring products from the interior to market,
   a. led to a sharp decline in canal building.
   b. hindered the development of railroads in the South and West.
   c. brought the West into the national economy.
   d. led to a decline in the port cities of the Northeast.

4. Improved transportation and the expansion of urban markets for northwestern produce between 1820 and 1860
   a. undermined the old alliance between the West and South.
   b. created a bitter rivalry between the Northeast and Northwest.
   c. posed a threat to the industrial economy of the Northeast
   d. limited growth of cities in the Northeast

5. The Waltham System
   a. was a new method of transportation.
   b. provided housing and education for textiles workers.
   c. was ultimately an embarrassment to Samuel Waltham.
   d. was the brainchild of DeWitt Clinton.

6. Which invention is incorrectly paired?
   a. Eli Whitney—cotton gin
   b. Oliver Evans—first American steam engine
   c. Cyrus McCormick—steamboat
   d. Samuel Colt—revolver

7. Factories greatly increased in the 1840s because of the widespread adoption of
   a. power from streams and rivers.
   b. steampower.
   c. mass production and interchangeable parts.
   d. cheap Asian labor.

8. The term "Let us conquer space" referred to
   a. the westward movement.
   b. the Indian wars.
   c. the Transportation Revolution.
   d. the Monroe Doctrine.

9. Critical to the collapse of the Federalist Party was the
   a. Transportation Revolution.
   b. Hartford Convention.
   c. Battle of New Orleans.
   d. invention of the cotton gin.

10. The Tariff of 1816
    a. dramatically reduced tariff rates.
    b. eliminated all tariffs.
    c. significantly increased tariff rates.
    d. made little change in existing tariff rates.

Matching Questions

For questions 11 through 15, use one of the lettered items.

11. Prohibited states from taxing federal property.___
12. Upheld the right of the Supreme Court to review all cases from state courts as long as they involved "federal questions."___
13. Guaranteed the sanctity of contracts by declaring unconstitutional a Georgia law rescinding a corrupt land sale.___
14. Upheld the right of the federal government to regulate interstate commerce.___
15. Upheld the contract clause by limiting the power of states to regulate private corporations.___

   a. *McCulloch v. Maryland*
   b. *Gibbons v. Ogden*
   c. *Fletcher v. Peck*
   d. *Dartmouth College v. Woodward*
   e. *Cohens v. Virginia*

For questions 16 through 20, use one of the lettered items.

16. Inventor of the steamboat.___
17. Leader of the Second Bank of the United States.___
18. Responsible for the idea of "interchangeable parts.___
19. The secretary of the treasury who proposed development of an elaborate system of internal improvements.___
20. Responsible for development of the Waltham System.___

   a. Robert Fulton
   b. Eli Whitney
   c. Nicholas Biddle
   d. Albert Gallatin
   e. Francis Cabot Lowell

True-False Questions

21. Excessive land speculation was one cause of the Panic of 1819.___
22. The Panic of 1826 was more severe than the Panic of 1819.___
23. The Erie Canal was one of the most important single improvements in the history of American transportation.___
24. The Waltham System was actually a factory community that completely managed the lives of its female workers.___
25. Evangelical religion had nothing to do with the rise of an industrial system in the United States.___

Essay Questions

1. The transportation and communications revolutions of the first half of the nineteenth century fundamentally changed the face of America and the habits of her people. Many "futurists" now believe that we are currently on the verge of another revolution that once again promises momentous changes, some similar to those of the nineteenth century but others even more dramatic. The chief forces of this new revolution also pertain to transportation and communications: nuclear energy, space exploration, and computer systems. What changes in society followed the nineteenth-century revolution?

2. What was the relationship between industrialism and evangelical religion?

_____

_____

_____

_____

_____

_____

_____

_____

_____

_____

_____

_____

_____

_____

_____

_____

_____

3. What are tariff duties? Why were they introduced in the Tariff of 1816?

_____

_____

_____

_____

_____

_____

_____

_____

_____

_____

_____

_____

_____

_____

_____

Self-Test Answers

1. a 2. c 3. c 4. a 5. b 6. c 7. a 8. c 9. b 10. c 11. a 12. e
13. c 14. b 15. d 16. a 17. c 18. b 19. d 20. e 21. T 22. F
23. T 24. T 25. F

SECTIONALISM AND PARTY 1816–1828

SUGGESTED OUTCOMES

After studying Chapter 9, you should be able to
1. Explain the westward movement of the early 1800s.
2. Explain how the issues of slavery, land, and transportation divided the North and the South in the 1820s and 1830s.
3. Explain why the invention of the cotton gin caused the cotton industry to boom in the early 1800s.
4. Describe the controversy surrounding the admission of Missouri into the union and how it was settled.
5. Explain the significance of the Denmark Vesey conspiracy.
6. Describe the treaties and foreign policy initiatives that established American boundaries and asserted American dominance of the continental United States.
7. Explain the significance of the Monroe Doctrine.
8. Explain why the presidential election of 1824 is considered one of the most controversial in United States history.
9. Describe the successes and failures of the John Quincy Adams Administration.
10. Describe the meaning of the term "Second Party System."
11. Explain the significance of the election of 1828.
12. Explain the meaning of the phrase "Rise of the Common Man."
13. Explain why the South opposed high tariffs.

CHRONOLOGY

1787 The Northwest Ordinance prohibits slavery in the Northwest Territory.

1793 Eli Whitney perfects the cotton gin.

1803 South Carolina reopens its foreign slave trade.

1808 Constitutional ban on importation of slaves takes effect.

1811 John Jacob Astor establishes fur-trading post in Oregon.
Henry Clay becomes Speaker of the House.

1817 John Quincy Adams becomes secretary of state.
The Rush-Bagot Agreement is signed.

1818 Treaty of 1818 is signed with Great Britain.
Andrew Jackson and U.S. troops invade Florida.

1819 The Adams-Onis Treaty is concluded.
Spain cedes Florida to the United States.
The Missouri controversy begins with the Tallmadge Amendment.

1820 The Missouri Compromise is reached.
Congress passes the Land Act.

1822 The Denmark Vesey conspiracy is discovered.

1823 President James Monroe issues the Monroe Doctrine.

1824 In the controversial election of 1824, John Quincy Adams becomes the sixth President of the United States.

1825 The Panama Congress convenes.

PHOTOGRAPH AND ILLUSTRATION ANALYSIS

1. Look at the accompanying painting. How does it glorify the westward expansion of the United States? How does it relate to the idea of Manifest Destiny?

_____

_____

_____

_____

_____

_____

_____

_____

_____

_____

_____

_____

_____

_____

_____

_____

John Gast's rendition of Manifest Destiny shows Indians and wild animals skulking off before the advance of westward expansion embodied in Columbia's stringing telegraph wires across the continent. *(Courtesy, Library of Congress, ca. 1862)*

NAME _____ DATE _____

MAP ANALYSIS

1. Look at the Missouri Compromise map. Why was Texas never considered part of the Missouri Compromise? Are Kansas and Nebraska north of the Missouri Compromise line?

_____
_____
_____
_____
_____
_____
_____
_____
_____
_____

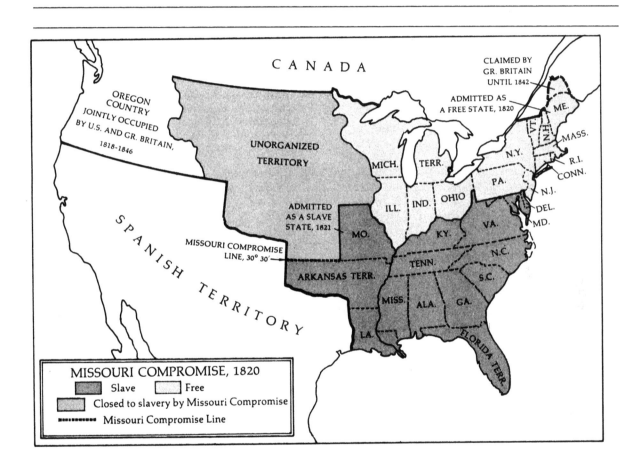

VOCABULARY

The following words may not be part of your normal vocabulary. If their meaning is not familiar to you, you should look them up in a dictionary.

domicile	ethos	tariff	egalitarian
travail	benevolent	conciliation	
libertarian	impunity	amelioration	
irony	caucus	despotism	

IDENTIFICATION OF KEY CONCEPTS

In two to three sentences, identify each of the following:

internal improvements _____
_____
_____

cotton gin and the revival of slavery_____
_____
_____

Tallmadge Amendment _____
_____
_____

Missouri Compromise _____
_____
_____

Treaty of 1818_____
_____
_____

Adams-Onis Treaty_____
_____
_____

Monroe Doctrine _____
_____
_____

Election of 1824 _____
_____
_____

American System _____
_____
_____

Panama Congress _____
_____
_____

Spoils System _____
_____
_____
_____

Election of 1828 _____
_____
_____
_____

Second Party System _____
_____
_____
_____

IDENTIFICATION OF KEY INDIVIDUALS

In two to three sentences, identify each of the following:

James Monroe_____
_____
_____
_____

James Tallmadge, Jr. _____
_____
_____
_____

William Crawford_____
_____
_____
_____

John Quincy Adams _____
_____
_____
_____

Denmark Vesey _____
_____
_____
_____

Henry Clay _____
_____
_____
_____

SELF-TEST
Multiple-Choice Questions

1. Southern lawmakers responded to the Vesey Conspiracy by
   a. enacting more humanitarian slave laws.
   b. open debate on the slavery issue in Congress.
   c. outlawing the distribution of antislavery propaganda.
   d. demanding reconsideration of the Missouri Compromise.

2. Andrew Jackson's policy of giving government jobs to his political supporters was known as
   a. the Spoils System.
   b. the Jackson Doctrine.
   c. the Monroe Doctrine.
   d. the Vesey arrangement.

3. Henry Clay's American System was all of these except
   a. the nation's first political campaign platform.
   b. an attempt to go back to pure Jeffersonian ideas.
   c. an attempt to modernize Jeffersonian ideas of government.
   d. a plan to improve the national transportation network under federal direction.

4. The winner of the election of 1828 was
   a. John Quincy Adams.
   b. Henry Clay.
   c. Andrew Jackson.
   d. William Crawford.

5. Eli Whitney's cotton gin
   a. allowed the cheapness of cotton following the War of 1812 to threaten the growth of slavery.
   b. restored slavery to profitability.
   c. had no application outside the South.
   d. made its inventor a fortune.

6. A central figure in the passage of the Missouri Compromise was
   a. John C. Calhoun.
   b. Daniel Webster.
   c. Abraham Lincoln.
   d. Henry Clay.

7. The Monroe Doctrine was
   a. an effort to make the American states a cooperative system.
   b. a bold assertion of American nationalism.
   c. a line drawn in the sands of the free state of Texas.
   d. a piece of Federalist campaign rhetoric.

8. Candidates in the election of 1824 included all but
   a. John Quincy Adams.
   b. William Crawford.
   c. Henry Clay.
   d. Daniel Webster.

9. The alleged corrupt bargain John Quincy Adams was charged with making concerned appointing
   a. Henry Clay to be his Vice President.
   b. Andrew Jackson to be his secretary of war.
   c. John Randolph to be his ambassador to South Carolina.
   d. Henry Clay to be his secretary of state.

10. The President who argued for national roads and canals, a national university, and federally-supported astronomical observatories was
    a. James Monroe.
    b. John Quincy Adams.
    c. Andrew Jackson.
    d. James Madison.

Matching Questions

For questions 11 through 15, use one of the lettered items.

11. Prohibited future European colonization in the Western Hemisphere.___
12. Provided for the cession of Florida by Spain to the United States.___
13. British-American treaty establishing the northwest boundary between the United States and Canada.___
14. Provided for British and American limits on naval forces on the Great Lakes.___
15. Henry Clay's program for high tariffs, internal improvements, and a national bank.___

a. American System
b. Monroe Doctrine
c. Adams-Onis Treaty
d. Treaty of 1818
e. Rush-Bagot Agreement of 1817

For questions 16 through 20, use one of the lettered items.

16. Although he had the largest popular vote, he lost the presidential election of 1824.___
17. Leader of a failed slave conspiracy.___
18. The President who argued for national roads, a national university, and a national observatory.___
19. Inventor of the cotton gin.___
20. The man credited with working out the Missouri Compromise of 1820.___

a. Henry Clay
b. Eli Whitney
c. Denmark Vesey
d. John Quincy Adams
e. Andrew Jackson

True-False Questions

21. The Denmark Vesey conspiracy was hardly noticed by whites.___
22. The Missouri Compromise allowed Missouri and Maine to enter the union as free states.___
23. The cotton gin was responsible for the revival of slavery.___
24. The Panama Conference was ultimately a failure.___
25. The Tallmadge Amendment would have prohibited slavery in Missouri.___

Essay Questions

1. What impact did the Vesey conspiracy have upon the South?

_____
_____
_____
_____
_____
_____
_____
_____
_____
_____
_____
_____
_____

2. How did the elections of 1824 and 1828 contribute to the emergence of the Second Party System?

_____

_____

_____

_____

_____

_____

_____

_____

_____

_____

_____

_____

_____

_____

_____

_____

_____

_____

_____

_____

3. What was Henry Clay's "American System" and how did it affect American politics in the 1820s?

_____

_____

_____

_____

_____

_____

_____

_____

_____

_____

_____

_____

_____

Self-Test Answers

1. c 2. a 3. c 4. c 5. b 6. d 7. b 8. d 9. d 10. b 11. b 12. c 13. d 14. e 15. a 16. e 17. c 18. d 19. b 20. a
21. F 22. F 23. T 24. T 25. T

THE JACKSONIAN ERA 1828–1840

SUGGESTED OUTCOMES

After studying Chapter 10, you should be able to
1. Describe American Indian policy during the 1830s and 1840s.
2. Explain why Andrew Jackson's inaugural party symbolized the "rise of the common man."
3. Place the Webster-Hayne debate in the larger context of land and states' rights.
4. Describe the development of the states' rights philosophy during the Jackson Administration.
5. Describe the nullification controversy and explain its political significance.
6. Explain the significance of the "Tariff of Abominations."
7. Describe how and why Andrew Jackson destroyed the Second Bank of the United States.
8. Explain the causes of the panic and depression that settled on America in the late 1830s and early in the 1840s.
9. Compare and contrast the philosophies of the Democratic and Whig parties.
10. Describe the major elements of American foreign policy during the Jacksonian era.

CHRONOLOGY

1828 John C. Calhoun anonymously writes the *South Carolina Exposition and Protest*.
Congress passes the Tariff of Abominations.
Andrew Jackson is elected President.

1830 Andrew Jackson vetoes the Maysville Road Bill.
The Anti-Masonic Party is organized.
The Webster-Hayne debate occurs.
Congress passes the Indian Removal Act.

1831 Nat Turner's slave rebellion terrorizes Virginia.
The Supreme Court decides the *Cherokee Nation v. Georgia* case.

1832 Andrew Jackson's crusade against the Second Bank of the United States begins.
The nullification convention meets in South Carolina.
Andrew Jackson is reelected to a second term.
The Bad Axe Massacre occurs.
The Supreme Court decides the *Worcester v. Georgia* case.

1833 Congress passes legislation providing for gradual tariff reductions.
Congress passes the Force Bill.

1835 The Seminole War begins.
Implementation of the Indian removal policy begins.

1836 Andrew Jackson issues his Specie Circular.
Martin Van Buren is elected President of the United States.

1837 The Panic of 1837 occurs.
The Supreme Court decides the *Charles River Bridge* case.
The *Caroline* affair occurs.

1838 The Aroostook War occurs.
The "Trail of Tears" begins for the Cherokees.

1840 Congress passes the Independent Treasury Act.
William Henry Harrison is elected President of the United States.

PHOTOGRAPH AND ILLUSTRATION ANALYSIS

1. Look at the accompanying painting. In what ways—positive or negative—does "The Verdict of the People" portray the rise of Jacksonian democracy?

_____

_____

_____

_____

_____

_____

_____

_____

_____

_____

_____

_____

_____

_____

The Verdict of the People, by George Caleb Bingham. Americans of the 1830s widely linked Andrew Jackson with the rise of the common man, though both the number of voters and the number of elective offices had been increasing for decades. (*Courtesy, Collection of the Boatmen's National Bank of St. Louis*)

114

2. Describe the historical background behind the painting "The Trail of Tears."

_____

_____

_____

_____

_____

_____

_____

_____

_____

_____

_____

_____

_____

_____

_____

_____

The Trail of Tears, by Robert Lindneux. Jackson disregarded the Supreme Court ruling that the Cherokees of Georgia had a right to their land. Many perished when they moved west on "the trail of tears." *(Courtesy, Woolaroc Museum)*

3. In what ways is this political cartoon critical of the South's role in the nullification controversy of 1832.

_____

_____

_____

_____

_____

_____

_____

_____

_____

_____

The Nullification Crisis threatened to tear the Union apart. This 1833 cartoon supporting Jackson portrays the South Carolina resolution as leading to civil war and despotism. *(Courtesy, The New York Public Library, Astor, Lenox and Tilden Foundations)*

VOCABULARY

The following words may not be part of your normal vocabulary. If their meaning is not familiar to you, you should look them up in a dictionary.

ardent	sovereign	precocious	injunction
patrician	diminutive	specie	insurrection
egalitarian	constructionist	speculative	
patronage	rescind	bankruptcy	
laissez-faire	incessant	default	

IDENTIFICATION OF KEY CONCEPTS

In two to three sentences, identify each of the following:

Charles River Bridge Case (1837) _____

_____

_____

_____

Webster-Hayne Debate _____

_____

_____

_____

Nullification Controversy _____

_____

_____

_____

Tariff of Abominations _____

_____

_____

_____

Indian Removal Act _____

_____

_____

_____

"Trail of Tears" _____

_____

_____

_____

The Bank War_____

_____

_____

_____

Cherokee Nation _____

_____

_____

Locofocos _____

_____

_____

Whig Party _____

_____

_____

Election of 1840 _____

_____

_____

Independent Treasury _____

_____

_____

Amistad Incident _____

_____

_____

IDENTIFICATION OF KEY INDIVIDUALS

In two to three sentences, identify each of the following:

Nat Turner _____

_____

_____

Andrew Jackson _____

_____

_____

Peggy Eaton _____

_____

_____

Robert Y. Hayne _____

_____

_____

_____

John Tyler _____

_____

_____

_____

Roger B. Taney _____

_____

_____

_____

William Henry Harrison _____

_____

_____

_____

SELF-TEST

Multiple-Choice Questions

1. The Whig Party often drew support from
    a. people favoring aid for internal improvements financed through a high tariff and higher prices for western lands.
    b. people who opposed a national bank.
    c. Irish and German Catholics.
    d. followers of Martin Van Buren.

2. The leading figure behind the nullification movement in South Carolina was
    a. John C. Calhoun.
    c. Andrew Jackson.
    b. Daniel Webster.
    d. Roger B. Taney.

3. The doctrine of nullification asserted
    a. the ability of the people as a whole to nullify acts of Congress.
    b. the power of the federal government to override objections of individual states to policies intended for the good of the nation.
    c. the right of an individual state to void any act of Congress it considered unconstitutional.
    d. the right of a majority of states to override federal legislation.

4. The depression of 1837 was the result of all these factors except
    a. cheap money policies on the part of the government.
    b. reckless speculation.
    c. the destruction of the Bank of the United States.
    d. the requirement that all payments for public lands be made in specie.

5. Which tariff was known as the "Tariff of Abomination"?
   a. 1816
   b. 1824
   c. 1828
   d. 1832

6. The "Trail of Tears" refers to
   a. the slaughter of the Cherokees by Andrew Jackson.
   b. the movement west of the Cherokees when many perished en route.
   c. a poem by William Cullen Bryant.
   d. a protest march on Washington, D.C., by native Americans.

7. Which order of Andrew Jackson led to the Panic of 1837?
   a. the decision to raise the tariff
   b. the requirement that western lands be paid for in paper money
   c. the requirement that western lands be paid for in gold or silver
   d. the decision to expel the Cherokees

8. The Whig Party
   a. brought democratic manners and sentiments to a Hamiltonian concept of government and economics.
   b. was a reaction against the Rise of the Common Man under Andrew Jackson.
   c. failed to benefit from the shifts in the economy.
   d. nominated Martin Van Buren for President.

9. In the election of 1840 Van Buren was successfully portrayed by his opponents as a
   a. virtuous farmer who had been born in a log cabin.
   b. bloated aristocrat living in lavish splendor.
   c. tool of Andrew Jackson.
   d. corrupt public figure who had stolen from the Bank of the United States.

10. The Democratic splinter party of the late 1830s and 1840s that opposed all forms of monopoly was known as the
    a. Whigs.
    b. Anti-Masonic Party.
    c. Jacksonian Party.
    d. Locofocos.

Matching Questions
For questions 11 through 15, use one of the lettered items.

11. The Democrat who became President after Andrew Jackson in 1837.___
12. The Whig who won the presidential election of 1840.___
13. The chief justice of the Supreme Court.___
14. The head of the Second Bank of the United States.___
15. The South Carolinian who launched the states' rights movement.___

a. Roger B. Taney
b. Nicholas Biddle
c. John C. Calhoun
d. William Henry Harrison
e. Martin Van Buren

True-False Questions
16. Long before Andrew Jackson entered the White House in 1829, American political institutions were gradually becoming more democratic.___
17. Andrew Jackson's Indian policy had as its objective the extermination of all American Indians.___
18. The Webster-Hayne debate had much to do with foreign policy and very little to do with sectional politics.___

19. Andrew Jackson's war on the Second Bank of the United States had nothing to do with the Panic of 1837 and subsequent depression.____

20. In many ways, the nullification controversy in South Carolina in 1832 reflected the issues that would lead to the Civil War.____

Essay Questions

1. Andrew Jackson strengthened the authority of the presidency, arguing that since the President owed his office to the votes of the entire nation, only he expressed the will of the people most effectively. Such an argument has been revived by other strong Presidents. How did Jackson increase presidential powers? Do you think the argument has merit?

2. How did Jackson's destruction of the national bank affect America's economy? What should be the role of a central bank? How does our banking structure today operate to maintain economic stability?

_____

_____

_____

_____

_____

_____

_____

_____

_____

_____

_____

_____

3. Describe the development of the Democratic and Whig parties. From what groups did each draw support? In what ways do the policies and constituents of the Democratic Party of Jackson differ from the Democratic Party of today?

_____

_____

_____

_____

_____

_____

_____

_____

_____

_____

_____

_____

_____

_____

_____

_____

_____

_____

Self-Test Answers

1. a 2. a 3. c 4. a 5. c 6. b 7. c 8. a 9. b 10. d 11. e 12. d
13. a 14. b 15. c 16. T 17. F 18. F 19. F 20. T

AN AGE OF REFORM

SUGGESTED OUTCOMES

After studying Chapter 11, you should be able to

1. Explain the main ideas of the "Declaration of Sentiments" (1848).
2. Describe the history of voting rights in early America and how the political culture of the country changed during the Jacksonian era.
3. Explain the background and significance of the Second Great Awakening and religious developments in the first half of the nineteenth century.
4. Describe the origins and early history of the Mormons.
5. Compare and contrast the Mormons, Methodists, Millenarians, and Shakers.
6. Describe what is meant by the term "secular communitarianism" and cite the major communitarian experiments in antebellum America.
7. Describe what is meant by "social reform" in antebellum America, cite the major reform movements, and evaluate their successes.
8. Describe the social and legal condition of women in nineteenth-century America and explain the term "Cult of Domesticity."
9. Explain why so many Americans feared Mormons, Catholics, and immigrants during the first half of the nineteenth century.
10. Describe the major themes in American art and literature during the antebellum era.

CHRONOLOGY

1774 Ann Lee brings the Shaker religion to America.

1817 The American Colonization Society is formed.

1824 Robert Owen establishes the New Harmony community.

1829 David Walker writes "An Appeal to Blacks" calling for emancipation.

1830 Joseph Smith publishes the *Book of Mormon*.

1831 William Lloyd Garrison founds *The Liberator*.

1840 World Anti-Slavery Convention meets in London.

1841 Dorr's Rebellion occurs in Rhode Island. The Brook Farm community is established.

1843 William Miller predicts the Second Coming of Christ will soon occur.

1844 Joseph Smith is assassinated and Brigham Young assumes leadership of the Mormons.
Ralph Waldo Emerson publishes *Essays*.
The American Republican Association, or Know Nothing Party, is established.

1848 Women's Rights Convention meets in Seneca Falls, New York.

1850 Nathaniel Hawthorne publishes *The Scarlet Letter*.

1851 Herman Melville publishes *Moby Dick*.

1855 Walt Whitman publishes *Leaves of Grass*.

PHOTOGRAPH AND ILLUSTRATION ANALYSIS

1. Look at the feminist fashions pictured here. What did the fashions state or represent at the time?

_____

_____

_____

_____

_____

_____

_____

_____

_____

_____

_____

_____

_____

_____

_____

_____

_____

_____

Stanton and Amelia Bloomer shown wearing the daring loose "bloomers"—long full Turkish trousers of black broadcloth with a short skirt and Spanish cloak. (_Seneca Falls Lily_)

The DRUNKARD'S PROGRESS,

OR THE DIRECT ROAD TO POVERTY WRETCHEDNESS & RUIN.

Designed and Published by J.W.Barber, *New Haven. Com. Sept. 1826.*

Woe unto them that rise up early in the morning that they may follow Strong Drink . . . Isa. 5 C. 11v.

Woe unto them that are mighty to drink wine, and men of strength to mingle Strong Drink . . . Isaiah 5 C.22v.

Who hath woe? Who hath sorrow? Who hath contentions? Who hath wounds without cause? . . . They that tarry long at the wine. Prov. 23

The drunkard shall come to poverty. Proverbs. 23. Chap. 21 v. The wages of Sin is Death Romans. 6. Chap. 23 v

The MORNING DRAM.   **The GROG SHOP.**   **The CONFIRMED DRUNKARD.**   **CONCLUDING SCENE.**

The Beginning of Sorrow, Neglect of Business, Idleness, Languor, Loss of Appetite, Dulness and Heaviness, a love of Strong Drink increasing.

Bad Company, Profaneness, Cursing and Swearing, Quarreling & Fighting, Gambling, Obscenity, Ridicule and Hatred of Religion. The Gate of Hell.

Beastly Intoxication, Loss of Character, Loss of Natural Affection, Family Suffering, Brutality, Misery, Disease, Mortgages, Sheriffs, Writs &c.

Poverty, Wretchedness, a Curse and Burden upon Society, Want, Beggary, Pauperism, Death.

An 1826 caricature depicting the evils of drink. (*Courtesy, The New-York Historical Society, New York City*)

2. Analyze the above illustration "The Drunkard's Progress." What is its message and how is it conveyed?

_____

_____

_____

_____

_____

_____

_____

_____

_____

_____

_____

_____

_____

_____

DOCUMENTS ANALYSIS

1. Read the account of Priscilla Evans reprinted here. What was the "Zion" she was speaking about?

_____

_____

_____

_____

_____

_____

_____

_____

_____

_____

_____

_____

_____

_____

_____

_____

_____

_____

_____

_____

_____

PRISCILLA EVANS, *though pregnant, walked with a handcart made of hickory from Iowa to Utah. Her account reveals the religious and economic motives that drove the Mormons across the continent to the Great Salt Lake, religious freedom, and ultimately economic prosperity.*

We began our journey [from Iowa City to Utah] of one thousand miles on foot with a handcart for each family, some families consisting of man and wife, and some quite large families. There were five mule teams to haul the tents and surplus flour. Each handcart had one hundred pounds of flour, that was to be divided and [more got] from the wagons as required. At first we had a little coffee and bacon, but that was soon gone and we had no use for any cooking utensils but a frying pan. The flour was self-raising and we took water and baked a little cake; that was all we had to eat.

After months of travelling we were put on half rations and at one time, before help came, we were out of flour for two days. We washed out the flour sacks to make a little gravy. . . .

No one rode in the wagons. Strong men would help the weaker ones, until they themselves were worn out, and some died from the struggle and want of food, and were buried along the waywide. It was heart rending for parents to move on and leave their loved ones to such a fate, as they were so helpless, and had no material for coffins. Children and young folks, too, had to move on and leave father or mother or both. . . .

We were much more fortunate than those who came later, as they had snow and freezing weather. Many lost limbs, and many froze to death. . . .

We reached Salt Lake City on October 2, 1856, tired, weary, with bleeding feet, our clothing worn out and so weak we were nearly starved, but thankful to our Heavenly Father for bringing us to Zion. . . .

2. Carefully read the "Declaration of Sentiments." What are the major arguments it is making about women's rights?

_____

_____

_____

_____

_____

_____

_____

_____

_____

_____

_____

_____

_____

DECLARATION OF SENTIMENTS (1848)

When, in the course of human events, it becomes necessary for one portion of the family of man to assume among the people of the earth a position different from that which they have hitherto occupied, but one to which the laws of nature and of nature's God entitle them, a decent respect to the opinions of mankind requires that they should declare the causes that impel them to such a course.

We hold these truths to be self-evident: that all men and women are created equal; that they are endowed by their Creator with certain inalienable rights; that among these are life, liberty, and the pursuit of happiness; that to secure these rights governments are instituted, deriving their just powers from the consent of the governed. Whenever any form of government becomes destructive of these ends, it is the right of those who suffer from it to refuse allegiance to it, and to insist upon the institution of a new government, laying its foundation on such principles, and organizing its powers in such form, as to them shall seem most likely to effect their happiness. Prudence, indeed, will dictate that governments long established should not be changed for light and transient causes; and accordingly all experience hath shown that mankind are more disposed to suffer, while evils are sufferable, than to right themselves by abolishing the forms to which they were accustomed. But when a long train of abuses and usurpations, pursuing invariably the same object evinces a design to reduce them under absolute despotism, it is their duty to throw off such government, and to provide new guards for their future security. Such has been the patient sufferance of the women under this government, and such is now the necessity which constrains them to demand the equal station to which they are entitled.

The history of mankind is a history of repeated injuries and usurpations on the part of man toward woman, having in direct object the establishment of an absolute tyranny over her. To prove this, let facts be submitted to a candid world.

He has compelled her to submit to laws, in the formation of which she had no voice.

He has withheld from her rights which are given to the most ignorant and degraded men—both natives and foreigners.

Having deprived her of this first right of a citizen, the elective franchise, thereby leaving her without representation in the halls of legislation, he has oppressed her on all sides.

He has made her, if married, in the eye of the law, civilly dead.

He has taken from her all right in property, even to the wages she earns.

He has made her, morally, an irresponsible being, as she can commit many crimes with impunity, provided they be done in the presence of her husband. In the covenant of marriage, she is compelled to promise obedience to her husband, he becoming, to all intents and purposes, her master—the law giving him power to deprive her of her liberty, and to administer chastisement.

He has so framed the laws of divorce, as to what shall be the proper causes, and in case of separation, to whom the guardianship of the children shall be given, as to be wholly regardless of the happiness of women—the law, in all cases, going upon a false supposition of the supremacy of man, and giving all power into his hands.

After depriving her of all rights as a married woman, if single, and the owner of property, he has taxed her to support a government which recognizes her only when her property can be made profitable to it.

He has monopolized nearly all the profitable employments, and from those she is permitted to follow, she receives but a scanty remuneration. He closes against her all the avenues to wealth and distinction which he considers most honorable to himself. As a teacher of theology, medicine, or law, she is not known.

He has denied her the facilities for obtaining a thorough education, all colleges being closed against her.

He allows her in Church, as well as State, but a subordinate position, claiming Apostolic authority for her exclusion from the ministry, and, with some exceptions, from any public participation in the affairs of the Church.

He has created a false public sentiment by giving to the world a different code of morals for men and women, by which moral delinquencies which exclude women from society, are not only tolerated, but deemed of little account in man.

He has usurped the prerogative of Jehovah himself, claiming it as his right to assign for her a sphere of action, when that belongs to her conscience and to her God.

He has endeavored, in every way that he could, to destroy her confidence in her own powers, to lessen her self-respect, and to make her willing to lead a dependent and abject life.

VOCABULARY

The following words may not be part of your normal vocabulary. If their meaning is not familiar to you, you should look them up in a dictionary.

incensed	sect	polygamy	parochial
resurgence	celibacy	mesmerism	nativist
professionalism	proliferation	clairvoyance	lyceum
evangelicalism	eccentric	phrenology	
domesticity	collectivism	utopia	

IDENTIFICATION OF KEY CONCEPTS

In two to three sentences, identify each of the following:

communitarianism _____

_____

_____

_____

Dorr's Rebellion _____

_____

_____

_____

Second Great Awakening _____
_____
_____
_____

Shakers _____
_____
_____
_____

Mormons _____
_____
_____
_____

Millenialism _____
_____
_____
_____

Methodism _____
_____
_____
_____

New Harmony _____
_____
_____
_____

Brook Farm _____
_____
_____
_____

Oneida Community _____
_____
_____
_____

Temperance movement _____
_____
_____
_____

cult of domesticity _____
_____
_____
_____

Seneca Falls Convention _____
_____
_____
_____

IDENTIFICATION OF KEY INDIVIDUALS

In two to three sentences, identify each of the following:

Robert Owen _____
_____
_____
_____

Thomas W. Dorr_____
_____
_____
_____

Charles G. Finney_____
_____
_____
_____

Ann Lee_____
_____
_____
_____

Joseph Smith_____
_____
_____
_____

Brigham Young_____
_____
_____
_____

William Miller_____
_____
_____
_____

Fox sisters _____
_____
_____
_____

John Humphrey Noyes _____
_____
_____
_____

Horace Mann _____
_____
_____
_____

Dorothea Dix _____
_____
_____
_____

Susan B. Anthony _____
_____
_____
_____

Lucretia Mott _____
_____
_____
_____

Nathaniel Hawthorne _____
_____
_____
_____

Herman Melville _____
_____
_____
_____

Edgar Allan Poe _____
_____
_____
_____

Walt Whitman _____
_____
_____
_____

David Walker _____
_____
_____
_____

1. Many early women's rights leaders were
   a. Episcopalians.
   b. Mormons.
   c. Shakers.
   d. Quakers.

2. The Second Great Awakening of the early ninteenth century generally believed in
   a. perfectionism.
   b. a symbolic interpretation of the Bible.
   c. bringing the kingdom of God to earth.
   d. total immersion in an icy stream for baptism.

3. A reason the Shakers shrank in numbers was
   a. physical attacks from neighbors.
   b. their practice of celibacy.
   c. the conversion to Mormonism.
   d. their "shaking," which destroyed their health.

4. The preacher who worked at "circuit" or route covering a particular area was usually a
   a. Presbyterian.
   b. Baptist.
   c. Congregationalist.
   d. Methodist.

5. The Auburn prison system allowed
   a. solitary confinement of prisoners at all times.
   b. physical labor by day and individual confinement at night.
   c. parole and probation.
   d. short one-year sentences for good behavior.

6. A leader of the Hudson River School of American landscape art was
   a. William Sidney Mount.
   b. George Caleb Bingham.
   c. Thomas Cole.
   d. Robert Mills.

7. In the United States after 1830 there was a rapid growth in
   a. anti-semitism.
   b. anti-Catholicism.
   c. Congregationalism.
   d. portrait painting.

8. Brook Farm, New Harmony, and Oneida were
   a. stations on the underground railroad.
   b. sites for national political conventions.
   c. towns where fugitive slave riots occurred.
   d. attempts at creating model societies.

9. William Miller was a leader of the
   a. Oneida Community.
   b. Mormons.
   c. Shakers.
   d. None of the above.

10. The women's rights movement advocated all of these except
    a. increased educational opportunities for women.
    b. less restrictive woman's clothing.
    c. insistence on ladylike behavior.
    d. antislavery.

Matching Questions

For questions 11 through 15, use one of the lettered items.

11. Religious group that eventually migrated to Salt Lake City to escape persecution.___
12. Since Christ's return was imminent, they believed there was no need to have children, so they practiced celibacy.___
13. Believed Christ's second coming was scheduled for October 22, 1844.___
14. Believed in "complex marriage"—that all men were married to all women.___
15. The most powerful of the evangelical movements in the nineteenth century.___

a. Shakers
b. Mormons
c. Millerites
d. Oneida Community
e. Methodism

For questions 16 through 20, use one of the lettered items.

16. Leader of the public school movement.___
17. Leader of the women's rights movement.___
18. Leaders of fraudulent mesmerism and clairvoyance movements.___
19. Leader of the Oneida Community.___
20. Leader of the movement for mental health reform.___

a. Dorothea Dix
b. Horace Mann
c. Fox sisters
d. Susan B. Anthony
e. John Humphrey Noyes

True-False Questions

21. None of the antebellum reform movements had any success.___
22. All of the communitarian experiments proved to be successful.___
23. The women's movement first emerged out of the antislavery movement.___
24. By escaping to their refuge in the Salt Lake valley, the Mormons escaped persecution and prospered.___
25. Dorothea Dix was the leading abolitionist of her day.___

Essay Questions

1. Throughout history, reform movements, moral crusades, and religious enthusiasm have often seemed to cluster. Describe the various social and religious movements of pre-Civil War America.

_____

_____

_____

_____

_____

_____

_____

_____

_____

_____

_____

_____

2. Why do you think all of these movements arose at about the same time?

_____

_____

_____

_____

_____

_____

_____

_____

_____

_____

_____

_____

_____

_____

_____

_____

_____

_____

_____

_____

_____

_____

Self-Test Answers

1. d 2. a 3. b 4. d 5. b 6. c 7. b 8. d 9. d 10. c 11. b 12. a
13. c 14. d 15. e 16. b 17. d 18. c 19. e 20. a 21. F 22. F
23. T 24. T 25. F

12 WESTWARD EXPANSION: THE 1840s

SUGGESTED OUTCOMES

After studying Chapter 12, you should be able to

1. Explain what happened at the Alamo in 1836.
2. Explain the background to European immigration to the United States in the first half of the nineteenth century.
3. Compare farm life in the North with farm life in the South.
4. Compare slave labor in the South with factory labor in the North.
5. Describe the leading figures in the abolition movement and the clash of philosophies among them.
6. Describe the arguments southerners used to justify the existence of slavery.
7. Describe the controversy in antebellum America over the return of fugitive slaves.
8. Explain the meaning of the term "Manifest Destiny" and describe the process by which the United States acquired new territory in the West in the 1840s.
9. Describe the causes of the Mexican War and the provisions of the Treaty of Guadalupe Hidalgo.
10. Explain how and why the issue of slavery in the territories became so volatile and how it spawned new political parties in the United States.
11. Describe the major issues and candidates of the election of 1848.

CHRONOLOGY

1831 The Nat Turner slave revolt occurs in Virginia.

1833 The American Antislavery Society is established.

1835 The "Gag" rule goes into effect in the House of Representatives.

1836 Texas successfully rebels from Mexico, and after being refused admission to the Union becomes an independent republic.

1838 The *Caroline* incident creates tensions between the United States and Great Britain.

1840 Congress passes the Independent Treasury Act.
      William Henry Harrison is elected President of the United States.
      The Liberty Party is formed.

1841 William Henry Harrison dies and John Tyler becomes President.
      The *Creole* slave mutiny occurs.

1842 The Webster-Ashburton Treaty settles the United States–Canadian boundary dispute.
      The Supreme Court decides the *Commonwealth v. Hunt* and *Prigg v. Pennsylvania* cases.
      Congress passes the Tariff of 1842.

1844 The Senate rejects John C. Calhoun's bill to annex Texas.
      James K. Polk is elected President of the United States.

1845 Texas enters the Union as a slave state.
      The John Slidell mission fails to purchase New Mexico and California from Mexico.

John L. O'Sullivan coins the term "Manifest Destiny."

1846 The United States declares war against Mexico.

Henry David Thoreau writes his *Essay on Civil Disobedience*.

General Zachary Taylor invades Mexico.

The Oregon Treaty settles the boundary dispute between Great Britain and the United States.

1847 General Winfield Scott captures Vera Cruz and Mexico City.

1848 Gold is discovered in California.

The Free Soil Party is organized.

Zachary Taylor is elected President of the United States.

The Treaty of Guadalupe Hidalgo ends the Mexican War.

1849 The California gold rush begins.

1850 The Compromise of 1850 is negotiated.

Zachary Taylor dies and Millard Fillmore becomes President of the United States.

PHOTOGRAPH AND ILLUSTRATION ANALYSIS

1. See the accompanying illustrations from the *American Anti-Slavery Almanac*. What attitudes are portrayed in the pictures? Is there some exaggeration?

_____

_____

_____

_____

_____

_____

_____

_____

_____

_____

_____

_____

_____

_____

_____

_____

_____

_____

_____

_____

_____

_____

_____

_____

_____

Illustrations of the American Anti-Slavery Almanac for 1840.

"*Our Peculiar Domestic Institutions.*"

Northern Hospitality—New-York nine months law. [The Slave steps out of the Slave State, and his chains fall. A Free State, with another chain, stands ready to re-enslave him.]

Burning of McIntosh at St. Louis, in April, 1836.

Showing how slavery improves the condition of the female sex.

The Negro Pew, or "Free" Seats for black Christians. | *Mayor of New-York re-fusing a Carman's license to a colored Man.*

Servility of the Northern States in arresting and returning fugitive Slaves.

Selling a Mother from her Child.

Hunting Slaves with dogs and guns. A Slave drowned by the dogs.

"*Poor things, 'they can't take care of themselves.'*"

Mothers with young Children at work in the field.

A Woman chained to a Girl, and a Man in irons at work in the field.

Branding Slaves.

Cutting up a Slave in Kentucky.

Paid.   *Unpaid.*

The abolition movement was an integral part of the reform sentiment that began in the 1830s. It emphasized moral suasion rather than legal coercion. (*Courtesy, Library of Congress*)

137

2. In what ways does the painting reprinted here glorify the Anglo settlement of Texas?

_____

_____

_____

_____

_____

_____

_____

_____

_____

_____

_____

_____

_____

_____

Texas land titles were freely issued to colonists, here by Stephen Austin and Baron de Bastrop, representing the Mexican government. *(Courtesy, Southern Pacific Company)*

NAME _____ DATE _____

3. Explain the significance of this caricature.

_____
_____
_____
_____
_____
_____

Caricature of Davy Crockett. The celebrated Tennessee frontiersman fought for Texas independence. *(Courtesy, American Antiquarian Society)*

DOCUMENTS ANALYSIS

1. Read the selection from Thoreau's *Essay on Civil Disobedience*. What argument is Thoreau making?

_____

_____

_____

_____

_____

_____

_____

_____

_____

_____

_____

_____

_____

_____

_____

_____

_____

_____

_____

_____

ESSAY ON CIVIL DISOBEDIENCE (1846) *by Henry David Thoreau. Thoreau was ardently opposed to both slavery and the Mexican War.*

How does it become a man to behave toward this American government to-day? I answer, that he cannot without disgrace be associated with it. I cannot for an instant recognize that political organization as *my* government which is the *slave's* government also.

All men recognize the right of revolution: that is, the right to refuse allegiance to, and to resist, the government, when its tyranny or its inefficiency are great and unendurable. But almost all say that such is not the case now. But such was the case, they think, in the Revolution of '75. If one were to tell me that this was a bad government because it taxed certain foreign commodities brought to its ports, it is most probable that I should not make an ado about it, for I can do without them. When a sixth of the population of a nation which has undertaken to be the refuge of liberty are slaves, and a whole country is unjustly overrun and conquered by a foreign army, and subjected to military law, I think that it is not too soon for honest men to rebel and revolutionize. What makes this duty the more urgent is the fact that the country so overrun is not our own, but ours is the invading army.

If the injustice is part of the necessary friction of the machine of government, let it go, let it go: perchance it will wear smooth,—certainly the machine will wear out. If the injustice has a spring, or a pulley, or a rope, or a crank, exclusively for itself, then perhaps you may consider whether the remedy will not be worse than the evil; but if it is of such a nature that it requires you to be the agent of injustice to another, then, I say, break the law. Let your life be a counter friction to stop the machine. What I have to do is to see, at any rate, that I do not lend myself to the wrong which I condemn.

MAP ANALYSIS

1. Look at the accompanying map. The Mexican War resolved the disputed territory and gave to the United States all the land in the so-called Mexican Cession. What contemporary American states were once part of the cession and the disputed territory?

_____
_____
_____
_____
_____
_____
_____
_____
_____
_____
_____
_____

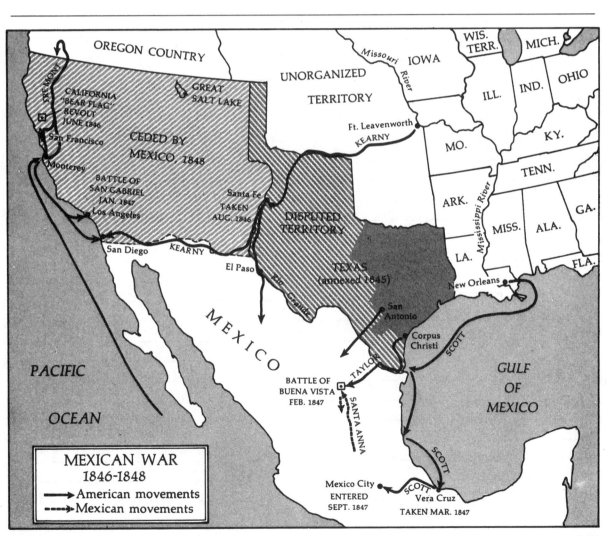

VOCABULARY

The following words may not be part of your normal vocabulary. If their meaning is not familiar to you, you should look them up in a dictionary.

carnage	repression	obstinacy	acrimonious
eradication	polemicist	mandate	stringent
complicity	genteel	insurgent	
laconic	extradite	proviso	

IDENTIFICATION OF KEY CONCEPTS

In two to three sentences, identify each of the following:

The Alamo _____
_____
_____

Abolition movement: gradual vs. immediate emancipation _____
_____
_____

The 1831–1832 Virginia debate over slavery _____
_____
_____

Gag Rule _____
_____
_____

Fugitive Slave Acts _____
_____
_____

Webster-Ashburton Treaty _____
_____
_____

Forty-Niners _____
_____
_____

Texas annexation _____
_____
_____

NAME _____ **DATE** _____

Young America _____
_____
_____
_____

The Oregon boundary question _____
_____
_____
_____

civil disobedience _____
_____
_____
_____

Mexican War _____
_____
_____
_____

Wilmot Proviso _____
_____
_____
_____

Treaty of Guadalupe Hidalgo _____
_____
_____
_____

Liberty Party _____
_____
_____
_____

"free-soilers" _____
_____
_____
_____

popular sovereignty _____
_____
_____
_____

Free Soil Party _____
_____
_____
_____

IDENTIFICATION OF KEY INDIVIDUALS

In two to three sentences, identify each of the following:

Sam Houston _____

_____

_____

William Lloyd Garrison _____

_____

_____

Theodore Weld _____

_____

_____

James Birney _____

_____

_____

James K. Polk _____

_____

_____

John L. O'Sullivan _____

_____

_____

Zachary Taylor _____

_____

_____

Nicholas Trist _____

_____

_____

John C. Calhoun _____

_____

_____

Henry Clay _____

_____

_____

Daniel Webster_____
_____
_____
_____

John Slidell _____
_____
_____
_____

SELF-TEST
Multiple-Choice Questions

1. Heroes of the Battle of the Alamo include all but
   a. Davy Crockett.
   b. Jim Bowie.
   c. William Barret Travis.
   d. El Degüello.

2. Which state was an independent nation before it became one of the United States?
   a. Rhode Island
   b. Vermont
   c. Florida
   d. Texas

3. The wave of immigrants in the early nineteenth century can best be charcterized as
   a. an influx of exploitable unskilled labor.
   b. threat to southern slavery.
   c. little different from earlier immigrations.
   d. a critical factor in the settling of the West.

4. In his *Essay on Civil Disobedience*, Henry David Thoreau opposed
   a. vegetarians and the imprisonment of criminals.
   b. the Mexican and Spanish-American Wars.
   c. slavery and the death penalty.
   d. slavery and the Mexican War.

5. The immigrants who experienced the *least* discrimination in the United States were the
   a. Chinese.
   b. Irish.
   c. Germans.
   d. English.

6. Support for the Mexican War came from
   a. Whigs such as Abraham Lincoln.
   b. the "continental Democrats."
   c. Henry David Thoreau.
   d. most antislavery spokesmen.

7. As a result of the Mexican War, the United States
   a. cleared its title to Oregon.
   b. annexed Texas.
   c. obtained California and New Mexico.
   d. extended the Missouri Compromise line to the Pacific.

8. Most free blacks
   a. strongly supported the goals of the American Colonization Society.
   b. objected to the goals of the American Colonization Society.
   c. encouraged deportation as the only recourse for enslaved blacks.
   d. considered themselves as foreigners on American soil.

9. Southern defenses of slavery rested on all of these except
   a. Biblical sanctions for slavery.
   b. the comparison of the condition of slaves with that of northern industrial workers.
   c. the assertion of black inferiority and need for assistance.
   d. the failure of the American Colonization Society.

10. Manifest Destiny rested on the assumption that
    a. expansion was the best method of settling the debate over slavery.
    b. all Americans supported expansion.
    c. the United States had a mission to civilize the continent.
    d. the dominant American sentiment for isolationism was dangerous.

Matching Questions

For questions 11 through 15, use one of the lettered items.

11. Settled the northern American boundary at the 49th parallel.___
12. Southern postmasters stopped the flow of antislavery literature into the South.___
13. Brought about the cession of California, Utah, Nevada, Arizona, and New Mexico to the United States.___
14. Compromise with Britain over boundary disputes.___
15. Prohibited slavery in any territories the United States acquired from Mexico.___

a. Wilmot Proviso
b. Treaty of Guadalupe Hidalgo
c. Gag Rule
d. Webster-Ashbuiton Treaty
e. Oregon Treaty of 1846

For questions 16 through 20, use one of the lettered items.

16. The influential abolitionist.___
17. The Liberty Party candidate who opposed the expansion of slavery.___
18. The military hero of the Mexican War who became President.___
19. The hero of Texas independence.___
20. Leader of the troops that attacked the Alamo.___

a. Sam Houston
b. Santa Anna
c. Zachary Taylor
d. James Birney
e. Theodore Weld

True-False Questions

21. The abolitionists rarely argued about what tactics to use in bringing about the end of slavery.___
22. The major cause of the Mexican War was Mexico's attempt to steal land from the United States.___
23. William Lloyd Garrison was among the most radical of the abolitionists.___
24. The most politically explosive issue in America during the 1840s and early 1850s was whether slavery should be permitted in the territories.___
25. Nat Turner instigated a slave rebellion in Mississippi.___

Essay Questions

1. Suppose you are a slave in 1853 on the Edwards plantation in Fort Bend County, Texas. You came to this spot ten years ago at the age of ten. Your former master fell on hard times and had to sell off a number of slaves including yourself, and you have not seen your parents for a decade. Tell about your life and the domestic slave trade seen by yourself. Describe your living conditions on the Edwards plantation. Have you married and do you have children? All and all, is life good or bad?

_____

_____

_____

_____

_____

_____

_____

_____

_____

_____

_____

_____

_____

_____

_____

_____

_____

_____

_____

_____

2. For many years, historians tended to condemn abolitionists as radical fanatics. More recently, younger historians have praised the abolitionists. How does perspective affect evaluation of the abolitionist movement? What contemporary movements draw upon the experience and tactics of abolitionists?

_____

_____

_____

_____

_____

_____

_____

_____

_____

_____
_____
_____
_____
_____
_____
_____
_____
_____
_____
_____
_____

3. Why did Southerners call slavery the "peculiar institution"?

_____
_____
_____
_____
_____
_____
_____
_____
_____
_____
_____
_____
_____
_____
_____
_____
_____
_____
_____
_____

Self-Test Answers

1. d 2. d 3. a 4. d 5. d 6. b 7. c 8. b 9. d 10. c 11. e 12. c
13. b 14. d 15. a 16. e 17. d 18. c 19. a 20. b 21. F 22. F
23. T 24. T 25. F

IMPENDING CRISIS: THE 1850s

SUGGESTED OUTCOMES

After studying Chapter 13, you should be able to
1. Explain the background and main ideas of Harriet Beecher Stowe's *Uncle Tom's Cabin*.
2. Discuss the controversy surrounding the Fugitive Slave Act of 1850.
3. Describe the successes and failures of territorial expansion in the 1850s.
4. Explain why the Kansas-Nebraska Act ignited such a political firestorm across the United States.
5. Explain why a civil war developed in Kansas during the 1850s and why many consider it a prelude to the larger American Civil War.
6. Explain why the Whig Party disintegrated and what the new Republican Party represented. What role did the expansion of slavery issue have in these political realignments?
7. Explain why many constitutional scholars consider the *Dred Scott* decision to be the most controversial Supreme Court decision in American history.
8. Explain the arguments on both sides of the Lincoln-Douglas debates.
9. Write the history of popular sovereignty from its rise in the late 1840s to its demise with the *Dred Scott* decision.
10. Explain the origins of the Republican Party.
11. Describe the outcome and significance of the election of 1860.

CHRONOLOGY

1850 The Compromise of 1850 is negotiated.
    Fugitive Slave Act goes into effect.
1852 Franklin Pierce is elected President of the United States.
    Harriet Beecher Stowe publishes *Uncle Tom's Cabin*.
1854 The Know-Nothing Party wins a number of political victories in the congressional elections.
    The Republican Party is founded.
    The Whig Party disintegrates.
    The Kansas-Nebraska Act is passed by Congress.
    Civil war begins in Kansas.
1856 John Brown conducts his raid at Pottawatomie Creek.
    James Buchanan is elected President of the United States.
1857 The Supreme Court reaches the *Dred Scott* decision.
    The Lecompton Constitution is ratified in Kansas.

1858 The Lincoln-Douglas debates take place.
1859 John Brown conducts the raid on Harper's Ferry.
1860 The Democratic Party splits into sectional factions.
    Abraham Lincoln is elected sixteenth President of the United States.
    South Carolina secedes from the Union.

PHOTOGRAPH AND ILLUSTRATION ANALYSIS

1. Look at the accompanying illustration. What is it describing?

_____

_____

_____

_____

_____

_____

_____

2. This painting portrays John Brown. How does the painting make him appear?

_____

_____

_____

_____

_____

_____

_____

John Brown, by John Steuart Curry. Following a raid against the free-state stronghold of Lawrence, Kansas, by proslavery men, Brown and his followers murdered five slavery sympathizers at Pottawatomie Creek. *(Courtesy, Kansas Industrial Development Commission, Topeka, Kansas)*

DOCUMENTS ANALYSIS

1. Read the following selection from *Huckleberry Finn*. What might Mark Twain have been saying in this portion of the novel?

_____

_____

_____

_____

_____

_____

HUCKLEBERRY FINN *by Samuel Clemens (Mark Twain). Huck talks about his feelings towards the slave Jim.*

. . . I about made up my mind to pray, and see if I couldn't try to quit being the kind of a boy I was and be better. So I kneeled down. But the words wouldn't come. Why wouldn't they?
. . . I was trying to make my mouth say I would do the right thing and the clean thing, and go and write to that nigger's owner and tell where he was; but deep down in me I knowed it was a lie, and He knowed it. You can't pray a lie—I found out.

So I was full of trouble, full as I could be; and didn't know what to do. At last I had an idea; and I says, I'll go and write the letter—and then see if I can pray. Why, it was astonishing, the way I felt as light as a feather right straight off, and my troubles all gone. So I got a piece of paper and a pencil, all glad and excited, and set down and wrote:

Miss Watson, your runaway nigger Jim is down here two mile below Pikesville, and Mr. Phelps had got him and he will give him up for the reward if you send.

I felt good and all washed clean of sin for the first time I had ever felt so in my life, and I knowed I could pray now. But I didn't do it straight off, but laid the paper down and set there thinking—thinking how good it was all this happened so, and how near I come to being lost and going to hell. And went on thinking. And got to thinking over our trip down the river; and I see Jim before me all the time: in the day and in the night-time, sometimes moonlight, sometimes storms, and we a-floating along, talking and singing and laughing. But somehow I couldn't seem to strike no places to harden me against him, but only the other kind. I'd see him standing my watch on top of his'n, 'stead of calling me, so I could go on sleeping. . . . and at last I struck the time I saved him by telling the men we had small-pox aboard, and he was so grateful, and said I was the best friend old Jim ever had in the world, and the only one he's got now; and then I happened to look around and see that paper.

It was a close place. I took it up, and held it in my hand. I was a-trembling, because I's got to decide, forever, betwixt two things, and I knowed it. I studied a minute, sort of holding my breath, and then says to myself:

"All right, then, I'll go to hell"—and tore it up.

---

2. Read the recollections of Thomas Henry Tibbles. How did John Brown feel about slavery?

_____

_____

_____

_____

_____

_____

THOMAS HENRY TIBBLES *was sixteen years old when he fought briefly with John Brown in "Bleeding Kansas."*

This Platte County, into which John Brown had invited me, was thickly settled. Though most of the houses were built of logs, there were a few fine frame residences. Also, behind these residences, there were always "nigger quarters," ramshackle stables, and loom-houses where Negro women wove the jeans and linsey-woolsey which formed the outer clothing of the whole population. The planters' wealth was made up of fine horses, "likely niggers," and a rich soil which produced immense crops of corn and hemp. Though many of the owners of this countryside could neither read nor write, they were proud and rich. How long John Brown had been secretly lingering there near his chosen rendezvous, or how many men he had with him, I never knew.

Night settled down dark and moonless. Clouds hung low in the west. I had difficulty in making my way to the appointed place, but there I found Brown. . . . [He] directed our group to go to a certain cabin belonging to a certain house and get the slaves who were expecting us. We all were to take them to the [Missouri] River by a road he described. Then the rest of our group were to take these Negroes over the river in skiffs that would be found at a designated place. . . . Brown said there was a regular road in front of the house where we were to get the Negroes, but that, as it was guarded by the planters' patrol, our party was to enter the farm from the rear and approach the slave quarters through a cornfield. He bade me go alone a mile up the direct front road to watch for the patrol and keep our main party informed of any danger from that source.

When I objected to dismounting and separating myself from my horse, Brown told me with a metallic ring in his voice: "You will obey orders." Doubtless if there had been more light, I should have seen a peculiar gleam in his eye. Anyone who had anything to do with Brown in Kansas learned that it was death, after one joined his band, to disobey any order he issued.

I went with his men as he had ordered. Because the night was so very dark, we had difficulty in finding the right place. I took my post in the bend, while the other men crept up through the cornfield. Just then the wind blew furiously and the rain poured down. I could see nothing except when lightning flashed now and then. Without warning someone threw his arms around me from behind, pinioning my elbows to my sides. Instantly two more men leaped upon me, but before they could clap a hand over my mouth, I uttered the loudest yell that had ever come of me. It was the only warning I could give my associates.

My captors tied my hands and feet; they put a rope around my neck and dragged me along the ground by it for some distance. Then they lifted me to my feet, threw the rope end over the limb of a tree. Just at that moment pistols flashed. Two of the men who had been holding the rope dropped to the ground; the other ran away. My "gang," who had succeeded in creeping up through the cornfield and bringing away two Negro men and one woman, had then overheard the rather loud talk of the patrol at my "hanging bee." Thanks to the black night and the rain, they had stolen up to us unnoticed.

They soon had me on my feet and helped me to find Old Titus and mount him.

Long before daylight it became obvious that the entire district was out on the warpath. Certainly John Brown's "nigger stealing" raid into Platte County had started a tremendous uproar. By now, however, probably all the rest of Brown's men were safely back across the river, and here was I, at sixteen, left alone to fight the whole county.

Just as day broke, I reached a dim lane that led toward the river. From sounds behind me I knew that not much over a mile away a large party was on my trail. . . . I leaped a fence into a cornfield—but they had seen me. I have never heard a more fiendish yell than they loosed then and there.

I plunged across the cornfield and finally reached the bottom lands of the river, which were covered in some places with grass as high as a man on horseback and in others with a dense growth of willows. My pursuers evidently had wholly lost my trail. My only way of escape was to swim to Missouri River with its rapid current, its rushing, mud-colored water, and its treacherous quicksands. After much thought I decided to take the risk. I led Old Titus down to the bank. I took hold of his tail and swam behind him; thus I not only relieved him of my weight, but was able to steer him wherever I wished. We landed [safely in Illinois] in a wild and desolate spot.

---

3. Look at the following letters regarding western settlement. What was life like in the western frontier?

_____

_____

_____

FILLING IN THE CONTINENT *These excerpts from a letter of Lucia Loraine Williams show that parts of the United States were far removed from the slavery controversy of the 1850s:*

September 16, 1851

Dear Mother,

We have been living in Oregon about two weeks, all of us except little John, and him we left twelve miles this side of Green River. He was killed instantly by falling from a wagon and the wheels running over his head.

After passing the desert and Green River [in present-day Wyoming] we came to a place of feed and laid by a day for the purpose of recruiting [resting] our teams. On the morning of 29 June we started on. John rode on the wagon driven by Edwin Fellows. We had not proceeded more than 2 miles before word came for us to turn back—we did so but found him dead. The oxen had taken fright from a horse that had been tied behind the wagon preceding this, owned by a young man that Mr. Williams had told a few minutes before to leave, and [the runaway team had] turned off the road. Two other teams ran also.

John was sitting in the back of the wagon, but as soon as the cattle commenced to run he went to the front and caught hold of the driver who held him as long as he could, but he was frightened and did not possess presence of mind enough to give him a little send which perhaps would have saved him.

Poor little fellow! We could do nothing for him, he was beyond our reach and O! How suddenly!

One half hour before we had left him in health as lively as a lark, and then to find him so breathless so soon was awful. I cannot describe to you our feelings.

We buried him there by the roadside, on the right side of the road, about ½ mile before we crossed the Fontonelle, a little stream. We had his grave covered with stones to protect it from wild beasts, and a board with his name and age. If any of our friends come through I wish that they would find his grave and if it needs, repair it.

[The letter proceeds to give excerpts from a diary of the trip.]

NEBRASKA

21 May—We had one of the worst storms that I ever read of. It beggars all description—thunder, lightning, hail, rain and wind. Hailstones so large that they knocked a horse onto his knees. The driver got out and held the oxen by the heads for they showed a disposition to run. Most of our things were completely soaked, so the next day we stopped and dried up.

On the 23rd we came to a creek that overflowed its banks, Elm Creek. The water was some 20 feet deep but not very wide. They fell a tree over the creek and packed the loading [across on foot], put our wagons into the water with a rope attached to the tongue, and swam them across.

June 1—Passed the Sioux village. Their wigwams are made of buffalo skins (the Pawnees' were mud). They seemed to be a much wealthier tribe than any that we [had] yet seen. The squaws were in antelope skins ornamented with beads; the men were also clothed with skins or blankets. They owned a great many ponies. On one of the wigwams were several scalps hung out to dry—taken from the Pawnees. They were friendly.

I saw some beautiful bluffs, apparently not more than ½ mile off, and wished to visit them. W consented to go with me but said that it was further than I anticipated. We walked 4 miles, I should judge, crossing chasms and bluffs before we reached the road and after all did not ascend the one we set out for. Camped by the Platte. No wood [to burn], but buffalo chips, which we have used for a long time.

WYOMING

On the 7th we arrived at Fort Laramie, and on the 8th commenced crossing the black hills. Some of them were steep. Laramie Peak to the left covered with snow.

9 June—Crossed the red hills and camped by a lake.

17 June—Traveled over 20 miles and camped by the Devils Hole, or Gate. In the morning two young ladies and myself visited it. The rocks on each side were perpendicular, 400 feet high, and the narrowest place was about 3 feet, where [the] Sweetwater came tumbling through. The road leading to it was crooked and thorny, but we found all kinds of beautiful flowers blooming beside the rocks; it was the most sublime spectacle that I ever witnessed

19 June—[Could] see the Rocky Mountains [at] a distance of some 60 miles. The tops were covered with snow, and from there they looked like fleecy clouds. Camped near two snowbanks in a beautiful valley.

IDAHO

2 July—[During the] night we were awakened by serenaders—five horsemen circled around the carriage singing "Araby's Daughter." It was a beautiful starlight night. We were surrounded by bluffs in a little valley, and on being awakened by their song, seeing their panting steeds and looking around upon the wild country, it seemed as tho we were transported into Arabia. They were beautiful singers from Oregon; said they were exiles from home. They sang "Sweet Home" and several others. Invited us to stay and celebrate the 4th. Said they would make us a barbecue, but we were anxious to get on and the affliction that we had just suffered unfitted us for such a scene.

31 July—Camped on the Snake. Indians came with salmon to sell. I let them have Helen's apron with a needle and thread and bought salmon enough for several meals. I wish you could [have eaten] with us. I certainly never tasted any fowl or fish half so delicious.

OREGON

3 September—Arrived at Milwaukie, and went into a house to live again, the first one that I had been in since we crossed the Missouri. . . .

If a nearby family's dinner in Oregon was typical, the journey was worth it:

Well We had Rosted Ducks . . . And Fat Chickens And Rosted pig and Sausages And green Apl pie And Mince pies and Custard pies And Cakes of difrent kindes [and] Inglish goosburyes And Plums Blue And green gages And Siberian crab Apples And oregon Apples. . . . Like wise Buter And Sturson pikles and Beet pickles And Sauce And Bread and Mashed potatoes and Oister pie And Coffe And Tea to be shore. Now I Must tel you What other preserves that I have. I have peaches And citrons And Sweet Aples, Crab Aples Jelley And Tomatoes And Mince And pairs and Aple Butter. And now I will Tel you of the Rest of My Winter Suplies. I have A plentey of Butter And Milk And a Thousand poundes of Salman And plentey Cabage And Turnips And A Bout A Hundred and Fiftey Bushel of potatoes And plentey of dried fruits—Aples and Black Buryes the Best that I evr saw. . . . I never Saw Sutch Black Buryes And Ras Bryes As There Is in this Countrey in All My Life Time. . . . O yes I Have plentey Shougar Laid in For Winter This Year Two. And Salt   (NEW YEAR'S DAY, 1852)

MAP ANALYSIS

1. According to this map, which regions of the South had the heaviest concentrations of slaves? Which regions had the least concentration? Why?

_____

_____

_____

_____

_____

_____

_____

_____

_____

_____

_____

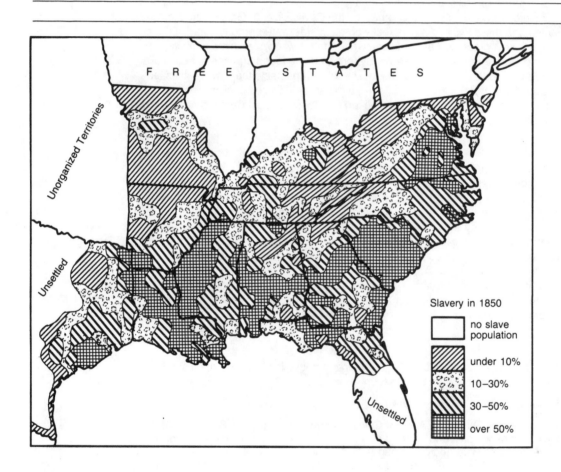

Slavery in 1850

- no slave population
- under 10%
- 10–30%
- 30–50%
- over 50%

VOCABULARY

The following words may not be part of your normal vocabulary. If their meaning is not familiar to you, you should look them up in a dictionary.

pious	paregoric	recrimination	polarize
bludgeon	pilgrimage	isthmian	travesty
ineffectual	ensconce	unsavory	coalesce
folklore	filibuster	militant	indolence

IDENTIFICATION OF KEY CONCEPTS

In two to three sentences, identify each of the following:

Uncle Tom's Cabin _____
_____
_____
_____

Fugitive Slave Act of 1850 _____
_____
_____
_____

Manifest Destiny _____
_____
_____
_____

Gadsden Purchase _____
_____
_____
_____

Ostend Manifesto _____
_____
_____
_____

Kansas-Nebraska Act _____
_____
_____
_____

"Bleeding Kansas" _____
_____
_____
_____

popular sovereignty _____
_____
_____
_____

Whig Party and the election of 1852 _____
_____
_____
_____

controversy over the transcontinental railroad _____

_____

_____

Pottawatomie Massacre _____

_____

_____

economic nationalism _____

_____

_____

Know-Nothing Party _____

_____

_____

Republican Party _____

_____

_____

Dred Scott case _____

_____

_____

Lecompton Constitution _____

_____

_____

Panic of 1857 _____

_____

_____

Lincoln-Douglas Debates _____

_____

_____

Freeport Formula _____

_____

_____

Election of 1860 _____

_____

_____

_____

IDENTIFICATION OF KEY INDIVIDUALS

In two to three sentences, identify each of the following:

Harriet Beecher Stowe_____

_____

_____

_____

Millard Fillmore _____

_____

_____

_____

Harriet Tubman _____

_____

_____

_____

Franklin Pierce_____

_____

_____

_____

William Walker_____

_____

_____

_____

Stephen A. Douglas _____

_____

_____

_____

John Breckinridge _____

_____

_____

_____

John Bell _____

_____

_____

_____

John Brown _____

_____

_____

_____

John C. Frémont _____

_____

_____

_____

Abraham Lincoln _____

_____

_____

_____

James Buchanan _____

_____

_____

_____

Hinton Rowan Helper _____

_____

_____

_____

SELF-TEST
Multiple-Choice Questions

1. The doctrine of popular sovereignty meant that
    a. ultimate authority rested with local governments.
    b. ultimate authority rested with federal government.
    c. voters in the territories should determine the status of slavery.
    d. only the national government could determine the status of slavery in the territories.

2. The *Dred Scott* decision held all of these except that
    a. slavery was unconstitutional.
    b. the Missouri Compromise was unconstitutional.
    c. black runaways were not citizens.
    d. Scott had no standing to sue in federal courts.

3. The Kansas-Nebraska Act
    a. reaffirmed the Missouri Compromise line.
    b. enjoyed the support of the Republican Party.
    c. settled the status of slavery in Kansas forever.
    d. shattered traditional political alignments.

4. The Fugitive Slave Law
    a. was upheld in most cases brought to court.
    b. enabled southerners to recover most runaway slaves.
    c. convinced most southerners that the North intended to comply with the Compromise of 1850.
    d. was declared unconstitutional in the case of an escaped slave named Shadrack.

5. The fundamental difference between Lincoln and Douglas concerned the
    a. economics of slavery.
    b. morality of slavery.
    c. constitutionality of slavery.
    d. issue of popular sovereignty.

6. The "Know-Nothing" Party
    a. was formed to counter the pro-immigrant American Party.
    b. was anti-foreign and anti-Catholic.
    c. remained neutral on slavery.
    d. never exhibited any political strength.

7. Southerners wished to acquire Cuba
    a. because it had a large and valuable slave population.
    b. for its ripe soil to farm cotton.
    c. because Spain was willing and eager to sell it at a reasonable price.
    d. for its coffee *fincas*.

8. The Whig Party declined in the 1850s because
    a. it was divided over the issue of slavery in the territories.
    b. its commercial programs were no longer attractive to the North.
    c. its leaders took intransigent positions on slavery.
    d. it supported a northern transcontinental railroad route.

9. In the Freeport formula Douglas acknowledged that as a practical matter
    a. Lincoln was right on the matter of competition between blacks and free white workers.
    b. territories could effectively exclude slavery.
    c. Southerners, as citizens, could take slaves anywhere they wished.
    d. personal liberty laws took precedence over the Fugitive Slave Act.

10. Candidates in the election of 1860 included all but
    a. John Bell.   c. Abraham Lincoln.
    b. John Breckinridge.   d. Frederick Douglass.

Matching Questions
For questions 11 through 15, use one of the lettered items.

11. An unsuccessful attempt on the part of the United States to purchase Cuba.___
12. Brought a section of what is today southern Arizona into the United States.___
13. Outlawed the Missouri Compromise line as a violation of Fifth Amendment property rights.___
14. Applied the popular sovereignty principle to a region of the United States which was north of the Missouri compromise line.___
15. Tried to bring Kansas into the Union as a slave state.___

a. Gadsden Purchase
b. Ostend Manifesto
c. Kansas-Nebraska Act
d. *Dred Scott* case
e. Lecompton Constitution

For questions 16 through 20, use one of the lettered items.

16. Leader of the raids at Pottawatomie Creek and Harper's Ferry.___
17. Author of *Uncle Tom's Cabin*.___
18. Leading figure in helping escaped slaves.___
19. The most prominent of the filibusterers.___
20. Argued that the plantation system impoverished most southern whites.___

a. William Walker
b. Harriet Tubman
c. Hinton Rowan Helper
d. Harriet Beecher Stowe
e. John Brown

True-False Questions

21. The *Dred Scott* decision virtually destroyed the popular sovereignty principle.___
22. The Panic of 1857 convinced southerners that their way of life was superior to that of the North.___
23. Unlike Stephen Douglas, Abraham Lincoln did not believe that slavery was morally wrong.___
24. The Compromise of 1850 and the Kansas-Nebraska Act virtually destroyed the Democratic party and provided for the rise of the Whig Party to power.___
25. Southerners viewed the Republican Party as the epitome of all they feared.___

Essay Questions

1. Historians often try to avoid moral judgments, but the bloody Civil War has produced much historical moralizing about the 1850s. During the 1930s, many historians dismissed the conflicts of the 1850s as "needless" and condemned the political leaders as a "blundering generation." How do you view the issues and leaders of the 1850s? Were issues such as the expansion of slavery ones that should have been confronted by the nation?

_____
_____
_____
_____
_____
_____
_____
_____
_____
_____
_____
_____
_____
_____
_____
_____
_____
_____
_____
_____

2. Why did the status of slavery in Kansas become such a burning issue to people all over the nation during the 1850s?

_____
_____
_____
_____
_____
_____
_____
_____
_____
_____
_____
_____
_____

3. What were the main parts of the Compromose of 1850? State whether each gave an advantage to the North or the South. Do political compromises usually work or make a bad situation worse?

_____
_____
_____
_____
_____
_____
_____
_____
_____
_____
_____
_____
_____
_____
_____
_____
_____
_____
_____
_____

3. What modern works of literature or creative works from other media have had the dramatic impact on our recent history that *Uncle Tom's Cabin* had on the people of the 1850s?

_____

_____

_____

_____

_____

_____

_____

_____

_____

_____

_____

_____

_____

_____

_____

_____

_____

_____

_____

_____

_____

_____

_____

_____

_____

_____

_____

_____

_____

_____

_____

_____

_____

Self-Test Answers

1. c 2. a 3. d 4. a 5. b 6. b 7. a 8. a 9. b 10. d 11. b 12. a
13. d 14. c 15. e 16. e 17. d 18. b 19. a 20. c 21. T 22. T
23. F 24. F 25. T

 **A GREAT CIVIL WAR 1861–1865**

SUGGESTED OUTCOMES

After studying Chapter 14, you should be able to

1. Explain the significance of John Brown's raid on Harper's Ferry.
2. Describe the process by which the South seceded from the Union.
3. Explain why the North won the Civil War.
4. Describe the government of the Confederate States of America.
5. Explain the dispute at Fort Sumter and why it precipitated hostilities between the North and the South.
6. Explain the military strategies of the North and the South.
7. Explain why the early military conflict was a stalemate.
8. Explain the origins of the Emancipation Proclamation and why Lincoln issued it.
9. Compare daily life in the Union with daily life in the Confederacy.
10. Explain the significance of the election of 1864.
11. Discuss in what ways the Civil War threaten civil liberties in the North.

CHRONOLOGY

1860 Abraham Lincoln and the Republican Party win the election of 1860.
South Carolina secedes form the Union.

1861 The remaining states of the South secede from the Union.
Fort Sumter is fired upon.
The Battle of Bull Run occurs.
The *Trent* affair occurs.

1862 Ulysses S. Grant captures Fort Henry and Fort Donelson.
The battle of the *Merrimac* and the *Monitor* takes place.
George McClellan's Peninsular campaign brings Union troops to the outskirts of Richmond, Virginia.
Second Battle of Bull Run occurs.
Battle of Antietam occurs.
Lincoln issues a preliminary Emancipation Proclamation.

1863 Lincoln issues the Emancipation Proclamation.
Battle of Chancellorsville occurs.
Battle of Gettysburg occurs.
Battle of Vicksburg occurs.

Battle of Chickamauga occurs.
Battle of Chatanooga occurs.

1864 Grant assumes command of Union troops.
Battles of Wilderness, Spotsylvania, and Cold Harbor occur.
Lincoln is reelected to a second term.
Sherman conducts his march to the sea.

1865 Lee surrenders.
Lincoln is assassinated and Andrew Johnson becomes President of the United States.
The Thirteenth Amendment is ratified.

PHOTOGRAPH AND ILLUSTRATION ANALYSIS

1. Look at the accompanying photograph of John Brown and read about his life in the textbook. What type of individual do you think he was?

_____
_____
_____
_____
_____
_____

John Brown. *(Courtesy, Library of Congress)*

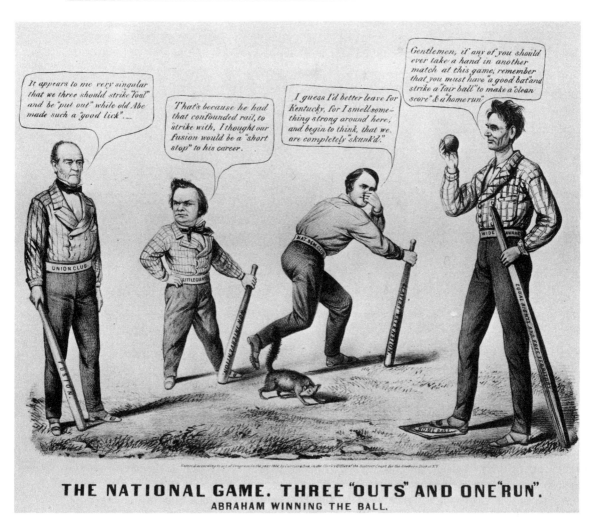

THE NATIONAL GAME. THREE "OUTS" AND ONE "RUN".
ABRAHAM WINNING THE BALL.

This cartoon employs a setting from the new game of baseball to argue that Lincoln won the 1860 election because he stood for equal rights and free territory. *(Courtesy, The New-York Historical Society, New York City)*

2. Explain this political cartoon.

_____

_____

_____

_____

_____

_____

_____

_____

_____

_____

_____

DOCUMENTS ANALYSIS

1. Read the southern diarist. How did her opinions change during the war?

_____
_____
_____
_____
_____
_____
_____
_____
_____
_____
_____
_____
_____
_____
_____
_____
_____
_____
_____

ONE SOUTHERNER'S DIARY ENTRIES, _for 1861 and 1865, tell the course of war:_

Saturday, July 13, 1861   Events transcending in importance anything that has ever happened within the recollection of any living person in _our_ country, have occurred since I have written last in my Journal. Since then _War_ has been declared. Our ministers sent North to negotiate terms of peace have been treated with cool indifference. Our forts are still retained with the exception of Sumter. _There_ the ever memorable victory was achieved which added fresh laurels to the glory of the gallant little state of South Carolina. Never shall I forget the state of intense excitement which pervaded the city of Augusta when it was announced that the fight was going on down at Sumter. Pa went down to Charleston just in time to witness from the top of the Charleston Hotel, the whole proceeding of the bombardment. It is needless to account the gallant achievement of Wigfall and others or to note the additional honour acquired by Gen Beauregard. . . .

Wednesday, March 29, 1865   I know I will regret hereafter that I have made no record of time and events which are fraught with so much interest, record of events which are hourly making history—but I cannot. I shrink from the task. At times I feel as if I was drifting on, on, ever onward to be at last dashed against some rock and I shut my eyes and almost wish it was over, the shock encountered and I prepared to know what destiny awaits me. I am tired, oh so tired of this war. I want to breathe free. I feel the restraint of the blockade and as port after port becomes blockaded, I feel shut up, pent up and am irresistibly reminded of the old story of the iron shroud contracting more and more each hour, each moment. I live too fast. A strange contradiction, yet true. A life of emotion, quick rapid succession of startling events will wear upon the constitution and weaken the physical nature. I may perhaps be glad hereafter that I have lived through this war but now the height of my ambition is to be _quiet_. . . .

VOCABULARY

The following words may not be part of your normal vocabulary. If their meaning is not familiar to you, you should look them up in a dictionary.

insurrection	venerable	benighted	provincialism
atonement	guerrilla warfare	demoralization	precarious
appease	loathsome	breach	
acquiescence	retrograde	gauge	

IDENTIFICATION OF KEY CONCEPTS

In two to three sentences, identify each of the following:

John Brown's Raid _____

_____

_____

_____

Fort Sumter _____

_____

_____

_____

Northern military strategy _____

_____

_____

_____

Southern military strategy _____

_____

_____

_____

Homestead Act of 1862 _____

_____

_____

Morrill Land Grant Act of 1862_____

_____

_____

_____

Abraham Lincoln and *habeus corpus* _____

_____

_____

_____

Copperhead Democrats _____

_____

_____

Battle of Bull Run _____

_____

_____

Battle of Gettysburg _____

_____

_____

Battle of Antietam _____

_____

_____

Battle of Vicksburg _____

_____

_____

Union blockade _____

_____

_____

Emancipation Proclamation _____

_____

_____

Election of 1864 _____

_____

_____

Republican economic policies during the Civil War _____

_____

_____

Ex Parte Vallandigham _____

_____

_____

Ex Parte Milligan _____
_____
_____
_____

Monitor vs. *Merrimac* _____
_____
_____
_____

IDENTIFICATION OF KEY INDIVIDUALS

In two to three sentences, identify each of the following:

William Seward _____
_____
_____
_____

John J. Crittenden _____
_____
_____
_____

Archduke Maximilian _____
_____
_____
_____

Jefferson Davis _____
_____
_____
_____

Ulysses S. Grant _____
_____
_____
_____

Robert E. Lee _____
_____
_____
_____

William Sherman _____
_____
_____
_____

George McClellan _____

_____

_____

_____

Charles Francis Adams_____

_____

_____

Stonewall Jackson _____

_____

_____

Joseph E. Johnston _____

_____

_____

Clement Vallandigham_____

_____

_____

_____

SELF-TEST

Multiple-Choice Questions

1. Secession as most supporters of the Confederacy viewed it was
   a. legally valid primarily because John Brown's raid was illegal.
   b. a revolutionary act, but essential to the preservation of southern society and property.
   c. necessary because after the election of 1860 the South could no longer control a majority in either house of Congress.
   d. a legitimate act by which the states resumed exercise of the sovereignty they had never surrendered to the federal government.

2. The problems faced by Confederate leaders included all of these except
   a. a chaotic railroad system.
   b. a lack of good generals.
   c. an underdeveloped economy.
   d. an unstable currency.

3. The Emancipation Proclamation affected slaves
   a. in all of the South.
   b. in all of the North.
   c. in all areas of both North and South.
   d. only in areas controlled by Union troops.

4. The so-called Copperheads were
   a. peace Democrats in the North.
   b. peace Republicans in the South.
   c. the avidly prowar activists in the South.
   d. the abolitionists.

5. Which of the following battles led to the Emancipation Proclamation?
   a. Antietam
   b. Gettysburg
   c. Vicksburg
   d. Atlanta

6. Basic northern strategy in the Civil War was to
   a. hold back and let the Confederacy starve.
   b. divide the Confederacy into two parts.
   c. arm the slaves.
   d. free slaves.

7. The southern states during the Civil War suffered from all except
   a. inflation.
   b. shortages.
   c. violent racial rebellions.
   d. the unavailability of many women workers.

8. Which were passed in 1862?
   a. Morrill Land Grant and Homestead Acts
   b. National Banking and Morrill Tariff Acts
   c. Emancipation and Second Confiscation Acts
   d. Davidson and Peabody Acts

9. During the Civil War Lincoln suspended the
   a. writ of habeas corpus.
   b. right of trial by jury.
   c. right of free press.
   d. right to use the mails to send newspapers with articles critical of the Union.

10. During the Civil War in New York City
   a. several blacks were lynched.
   b. mobs attacked dozens of government buildings.
   c. the mayor was killed by antidraft protesters.
   d. the *Merrimac* fired at downtown Manhattan.

Matching Questions
For questions 11 through 15, use one of the lettered items.

11. The naval standoff that brought on hostilities between North and South.___
12. Inspired Lincoln's famous speech.___
13. Allowed Lincoln to proceed with the Emancipation Proclamation.___
14. Gave Union forces control of the Mississippi River.___
15. The first major land battle of the Civil War.___

   a. Battle of Antietam
   b. Battle of Vicksburg
   c. Battle of Bull Run
   d. Battle of Gettysburg
   e. Battle of Fort Sumter

True-False Questions
16. The Homestead Act provided 160 acres of public domain land free to settlers who agreed to live on the land and make improvements.___
17. The Morrill Act of 1862 established our system of land grant colleges.___
18. The Battle of Antietam was a great Confederate victory.___
19. During the Civil War, the southern states suffered from inflation and shortages of essential items.___
20. The Emancipation Proclamation freed all of the slaves in America.___

Essay Questions

1. Why did President Lincoln react as he did to secession? Why did he not simply let the southern states go? What might have been the consequences?

_____

_____

_____

_____

_____

_____

_____

_____

_____

_____

_____

_____

_____

_____

_____

_____

_____

_____

_____

_____

_____

_____

_____

_____

_____

_____

_____

_____

_____

_____

_____

_____

_____

_____

_____

2. Historians have sometimes asked the question, "Was the Civil War, in terms of its results, worth the bloodshed and costs?" How would you answer this question? What is the value of asking such moral questions of the past?

_____
_____
_____
_____
_____
_____
_____
_____
_____
_____
_____
_____
_____
_____
_____
_____
_____
_____
_____
_____
_____
_____
_____
_____
_____
_____
_____
_____
_____
_____
_____
_____
_____
_____
_____
_____
_____
_____
_____
_____
_____
_____
_____

3. Given the strong antiblack feeling throughout most of the country in 1860 and the minimal support for abolitionism, why did northern men volunteer for the Union army? Given the fact that most southern whites did not hold slaves, why did so many men join the Confederate army?

_____
_____
_____
_____
_____
_____
_____
_____
_____
_____
_____
_____
_____
_____
_____
_____
_____
_____
_____
_____
_____
_____
_____
_____
_____
_____
_____
_____
_____
_____
_____

Self-Test Answers

1. d 2. b 3. d 4. a 5. a 6. b 7. c 8. a 9. a 10. a 11. e 12. d
13. a 14. b 15. c 16. T 17. T 18. F 19. T 20. F

15 "BEEN IN THE STORM SO LONG": EMANCIPATION AND RECONSTRUCTION

SUGGESTED OUTCOMES

After studying Chapter 15, you should be able to

1. Describe the economic and social condition of the South in 1865.
2. Identify organizations that helped or hindered emancipation.
3. Describe the impact of slavery and emancipation on African-American family life and on the social life of the larger African-American community.
4. Provide a brief, general definition of the meaning of the term "Reconstruction."
5. Explain the major provisions of the Abraham Lincoln, the Andrew Johnson, and the Radical Republican proposals for Reconstruction, and explain the significant differences among them.
6. Describe the Radical Republican proposal to provide farm land of their own to the recently emancipated slaves, and explain why the proposal was never implemented.
7. Explain the process by which Reconstruction came to an end in the various southern states, and provide an overall explanation for why Reconstruction came to an end in the South.
8. Provide a general explanation for why historians have been critical of the presidency of Andrew Johnson.
9. Trace the major achievements (civil rights bills and the Thirteenth, Fourteenth, and Fifteenth Amendments) of Radical Republicans in promoting civil rights.
10. Explain why Andrew Johnson almost lost the presidency in impeachment proceedings.
11. Explain why the united movement for African-American voting rights and women's voting rights split in the late 1860s.
12. Describe the various groups struggling for political power in the South during Reconstruction.

CHRONOLOGY

1863 Abraham Lincoln issues the Emancipation Proclamation.
Abraham Lincoln gives the Gettysburg Address.

1864 Ulysses S. Grant assumes command of the Union Army.
Abraham Lincoln wins a second presidential term.
Congress passes the Wade-Davis Bill.

1865 Congress establishes the Freedmen's Bureau.
General Robert E. Lee surrenders at Appomattox Court House.
Abraham Lincoln is assassinated and Andrew Johnson becomes President.
The Thirteenth Amendment to the Constitution is adopted.

1866 Congress passes the Civil Rights Act of 1866.
Tennessee is readmitted to Congress and the Union.

1867 Congress passes the Tenure of Office Act.
Congress passes the Military Reconstruction Act.

1868 Congress conducts impeachment proceedings against President Andrew Johnson.
The Fourteenth Amendment to the Constitution is adopted.
Ulysses S. Grant is elected President.
Alabama, Arkansas, Florida, Louisiana, North Carolina, South Carolina, and Georgia are readmitted to Congress and the Union.

1870	Texas, Mississippi, and Virginia are readmitted to Congress and the Union.
1872	Ulysses S. Grant wins a second presidential term.
	Congress passes the Amnesty Act.
	Crédit Mobilier scandal is exposed.
1875	Congress passes the Civil Rights Act of 1875.

| 1876 | The presidential election between Republican Rutherford B. Hayes and Democrat Samuel Tilden ends in dispute. |
| 1877 | The Compromise of 1877 is reached and Rutherford B. Hayes is declared President. |

PHOTOGRAPH AND ILLUSTRATION ANALYSIS

1. The accompanying photograph is a collective portrait of the African-American members of the Louisiana state legislature during Reconstruction. What role did African Americans play in southern state governments during Reconstruction?

_____

_____

_____

_____

_____

_____

_____

_____

_____

_____

_____

_____

_____

_____

_____

_____

_____

_____

_____

_____

_____

_____

_____

_____

_____

_____

_____

_____

Louisiana was one of five southern states to have a majority of black voters after the Civil War. A total of 133 black legislators served in the state from 1868 to 1896. *(Courtesy, Louisiana State Museum)*

179

2. Some northerners argued that the Civil War did not really do too much damage to the South. Using the accompanying photograph of Charleston, South Carolina, how would you react to that argument?

_____

_____

_____

_____

_____

Charleston, South Carolina. At the war's end, much of the South lay in ruins. (*Courtesy, Library of Congress*)

DOCUMENTS ANALYSIS

1. Read the following sharecropping contract. How did the contract actually trap the sharecropper into a legal and economic situation that resembled slavery?

_____

_____

_____

_____

_____

_____

_____

2. Distinguish between congressional and presidential Reconstruction. Was Reconstruction at least partially successful? In what respects, if any?

3. What does this testimony of Harriet Hernandes, a black living in Spartanburg, South Carolina, in 1871, reveal about the nature of Ku Klux Klan intimidation?

_____

_____

_____

_____

_____

_____

_____

INTIMIDATION OF BLACK VOTERS *The following testimony was given by Harriet Hernandes, a black resident of Spartanburg, South Carolina, July 10, 1871, to the Joint Congressional Select Committee investigating conditions in the South.*

Question: How old are you?
Answer: Going on thirty-four years. . . .

Q: Are you married or single?
A: Married.

Q: Did the Ku-Klux come to your house at any time?
A: Yes, sir; twice. . . .

Q: Go on to the second time. . . .
A: They came in; I was lying in bed. Says he, "Come out here, sir; come out here, sir!" They took me out of bed; they would not let me get out, but they took me up in their arms and toted me out—me and my daughter Lucy. He struck me on the forehead with a pistol, and here is the scar above my eye now. Says he, "Damn you, fall." I fell. Says he, "Damn you, get up." I got up. Says he, "Damn you, get over this fence!" and he kicked me over when I went to get over; and then he went on to a brush pile, and they laid us right down there, both together. They laid us down twenty yards apart, I reckon. They had dragged and beat us along. They struck me right on the top of my head, and I thought they had killed me; and I said, "Lord o' mercy, don't, don't kill my child!" He gave me a lick on the head, and it liked to have killed me; I saw stars. He threw my arm over my head so I could not do anything with it for three weeks, and there are great knots on my wrist now.

Q: What did they say this was for?
A: They said, "You can tell your husband that when we see him we are going to kill him. . . ."

Q: Did they say why they wanted to kill him?
A: They said, "He voted the radical ticket, didn't he?" I said, "Yes," that very way. . . .

Q: When did [your husband] get back home after this whipping? He was not at home, was he?
A: He was lying out; he couldn't stay at home, bless your soul! . . .

Q: Has he been afraid for any length of time?
A: He has been afraid ever since last October. He has been lying out. He has not laid in the house ten nights since October.

Q: Is that the situation of the colored people down there to any extent?
A: That is the way they all have to do—men and women both.

Q: What are they afraid of?
A: Of being killed or whipped to death.

Q: What has made them afraid?
A: Because men that voted radical tickets they took the spite out on the women when they could get at them.

Q: How many colored people have been whipped in that neighborhood?
A: It is all of them, mighty near. . . .

NAME _____ DATE _____

VOCABULARY
The following words may not be part of your normal vocabulary. If their meaning is not familiar to you, you should look them up in a dictionary.

renascent   coercive   suffrage   confiscate
gender   reconciliation   paternalistic   tenancy
antebellum   magnanimous   philanthropic   impeachment

IDENTIFICATION OF KEY CONCEPTS
In two to three sentences, identify each of the following:

Abraham Lincoln's plan for Reconstruction _____
_____
_____

Andrew Johnson's plan for Reconstruction _____
_____
_____

The Radical Republican plan for Reconstruction _____
_____
_____

Thirteenth Amendment _____
_____
_____

Fourteenth Amendment _____
_____
_____

Fifteenth Amendment _____
_____
_____

Military Reconstruction Act of 1867 _____
_____
_____

Freedmen's Bureau _____

_____

_____

Sharecropping _____

_____

_____

Wade Davis Bill _____

_____

_____

"Black Codes" _____

_____

_____

Carpetbaggers _____

_____

_____

Scalawags _____

_____

_____

Redeemers _____

_____

_____

Compromise of 1877 _____

_____

_____

_____

PHOTOGRAPHIC EXERCISE

1. Why might the engraving on the left on the following page, entitled "Verdict, 'Hang the D_ Yankee and Nigger,'" relate to the black suffrage convention of 1866 in New Orleans?

_____

_____

_____

_____

_____

_____

Matching Questions

For questions 11 through 15, use one of the lettered items.

11. Northerners who came the South to assist poor African Americans and to exploit the South economically.___
12. Conservative whites who took over the southern state governments at the end of Reconstruction.___
13. A term for white southerners who cooperated with northern officials during Reconstruction.___
14. Federal workers who tried to provide education and health benefits to the recently emancipated African Americans in the South.___
15. Northern politicians interested in punishing southern whites and in providing political rights to southern African Americans.___

a. Carpetbaggers
b. Scalawags
c. Freedmen's Bureau
d. Redeemers
e. Radical Republicans

For questions 16 through 20, use one of the lettered items.

16. Freed the slaves.___
17. Gave the recently emancipated slaves the right to vote.___
18. Resolved the disputed presidential election.___
19. Gave citizenship to African Americans.___
20. Imposed harsh terms on the former Confederate states.___

a. Compromise of 1877
b. Fourteenth Amendment
c. Military Reconstruction Act of 1867
d. Thirteenth Amendment
e. Fifteenth Amendment

True-False Questions

21. The Crédit Mobilier scandal occurred under President Lincoln.___
22. Abraham Lincoln's reconstruction plan was generally considered to be very harsh on the South.___
23. The most important leaders of Radical Reconstruction were Charles Sumner and Thaddeus Stevens.___
24. The crop-lien system often kept ex-slaves in perpetual debt.___
25. Andrew Johnson became president upon the assassination of Abraham Lincoln.___

Essay Questions

1. Was Reconstruction at least partially successful? In what respects, if any?

_____

_____

_____

_____

_____

_____

_____

_____

_____

_____

_____

2. Who really won the civil War—the North or the South? Consider all of the questions the war was fought over and explain your answer?

_____

_____

_____

_____

_____

_____

_____

_____

_____

_____

_____

_____

_____

_____

3. Did Susan B. Anthony, Elizabeth Cady Stanton, and the National Woman Suffrage Association support the Fifteenth Amendment? Explain the conflict involved for the woman's movement.

_____

_____

_____

_____

_____

_____

_____

_____

_____

_____

_____

_____

_____

_____

Self-Test Answers

1. b 2. d 3. b 4. a 5. c 6. d 7. a 8. d 9. b 10. a 11. a 12. d
13. b 14. c 15. e 16. d 17. e 18. a 19. b 20. c 21. F
22. F 23. T 24. T 25. T

NOTES

NOTES

NOTES

NOTES